D1055495

# Follow Me,
# I'm Right Behind You!

# Follow Me, I'm Right Behind You!

## Tom O'Connor

A Treasury of Irish Humour

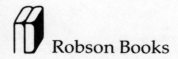

Robson Books

First published in Great Britain in 1995 by Robson
Books Ltd, Bolsover House, 5–6 Clipstone Street,
London W1P 8LE

Copyright © 1995 Tom O'Connor

The right of Tom O'Connor to be identified as
author of this work has been asserted by him in
accordance with the Copyright, Designs and
Patents Act 1988.

Book design by Harold King
Illustrated by Jim Hutchings

**British Library Cataloguing in Publication Data**
A catalogue record for this title is available from
the British Library

ISBN 0 86051 993 7

Photoset in Souvenir by Derek Doyle &
Associates, Mold, Clwyd. Printed in Great Britain
by Butler & Tanner Ltd, London and Frome.

For Joe –
You're always on my mind son

# Contents

# Introduction

It seems that in certain branches of comedy there has to be a butt to every joke. Whether it be race, colour, creed, even football preference or, worse still, a person of little intelligence, there must always be a loser.

Personally, I've never gone with this type of humour, realizing how awful it would feel to be the one person in the audience that the others were ridiculing. I knew that in turn, many races and nationalities have felt the barbs of the cynical gags – Jews, Pakistanis, Blacks, Poles. But surely the all-time fall-guys have been the Irish.

'Did you hear about the Irish feller who …'

'There was this Irish bloke …'

'An Englishman, an Irishman and a Scotsman …' (guess who always lost out in that one?)

On and on roll the dreary, stale old tales – providing entertainment for people who laugh only because the jokes are not about them.

With this book I decided to redress the balance a little. Whilst admitting that there are potty people the world over, just as there are highly intelligent folk, I've tried to look at Irish comedy through Irish eyes. Credit is given where due, and silliness is highlighted when it arises. But, overall, I've tried to demonstrate the one feature that separates the Gael from all other breeds – pure, natural wit, and the ability to find fun in even the darkest corner. 'So here we go' as my grandmother used to say. 'Single file in twos, spread out in a bunch and follow me, I'm right behind you!'

A wise man, or to be politically correct, a wise person, once said that Irish jokes are simple so that the English can understand them. Who knows how true that may be. What we certainly do know is that there is no finer wit than that from the Emerald Isle. There are no nicer folk than those gentle souls who dwell in the land of shining lakes, dark beer and 'true' tales of the little people.

This book contains some of my favourite Irish stories – some believable perhaps, others just an example of the lateral way that the Irish think at times. If you feel just a little happier after reading these pages then put it all down to a sign I once saw in the window of a pizza restaurant in Dalkey:

'Special opening offer: Buy one pizza for the price of two and get another completely free!!'

(The place was packed out – honestly!)

# 1

---

# The
# Irish
# at Work

'And man must work and women weep for ever and for ever.' Whoever said those words has never experienced a working man weeping whether they be tears of sadness or, more likely, tears of joy. Because one thing is for certain, without fun work would not be work, it would be slavery.

I've always maintained that the best job to have is one which you enjoy doing irrespective of pay or conditions, and this opinion is generally held by the world's most famous workers – the Irish labourers.

For without the working Irishman, what an under-developed world we would live in. From times as long ago as the days of ancient Egypt ('It must have been the Irish who built the pyramids 'cos no one else could carry up the bricks' said the wise man), the hard-working Paddy has played more than his part in the building, knocking down and general reshaping of every civilization.

'Rome wasn't built in a day, you know,' moaned the malingering bricklayer.

'Ah, but I wasn't in charge of that job,' retorted the Kerry-born foreman.

So, with worldwide thanks to the 'sons of toil from Erin's oisle' here are some tales of the Irish at work.

Murphy applied for the job as head chef at a very swish restaurant.

'Come to the kitchen and show us what you can do,' said the manager.

'Give me an egg,' said Murphy, 'any size, any colour' – and this was done.

In a trice, our hero grabbed the egg and threw it five feet in the air, caught it on the instep of his right foot, flicked it to his left foot, flicked it onto his left shoulder, shrugged it over to his right shoulder, shrugged it up to his forehead and gently nodded it towards a frying pan on a nearby cooker.

The egg hit the rim of the pan and broke, the contents oozing gently into the fat and the shell dropping into a waste bin.

'That's brilliant,' said the manager. 'Can you do it again?'

'Certainly, sir,' said Murphy, and duly obliged.

Staring at the two sizzling eggs and the shell neatly stowed in the bin, the manager remarked, 'That's the most amazing display I've ever seen.'

'Do I get the job then?' inquired Murphy.

'No,' said the manager, 'you mess about too much.'

While being interviewed for a job, the personnel manager said to the Maguire brothers:

'We're going to give you a written examination. Ten questions. Whoever gets most right we'll hire.'

Papers were produced and the boys set to work answering the general knowledge questions. When the time was up the personnel manager collected and marked the papers.

'Well,' said he, 'you've both got nine out of ten, but I'm giving Mick the job.'

'Why's that?' asked Pat.

'Well,' said the manager, 'you both got the same question wrong but he had 'I don't know this' and you had 'Neither do I'.

'The boss has been on the phone,' said Cassidy. 'He says they're sending down a thousand bricks this afternoon.'

'My God,' cried Kelly, 'how many bricks are in a thousand?'

'I don't know,' said Cassidy, 'but there must be millions!'

'You guys in the trench,' shouted the foreman. 'Can you climb out a minute.' And out they clambered.

'Stamp your feet as hard as you can,' he ordered. And they did.

'Now jump back into the trench, then jump out and stamp your feet again.'

'Excuse me, sor,' muttered O'Rafferty, 'would this be some kind of pagan ritual or such like?'

'No,' said the gaffer, 'you're bringing out more soil with your boots than you are with your shovels!'

Which reminds me of a not too longish tale of Casey's first day on the building site.

'Do you have any experience?' asked the site foreman.

'No,' remarked Casey. 'But bedad I'm strong in the back.'

'Good,' said the gaffer. 'You can start by carrying up bricks. It's hard work but I'm sure you're used to that.'

'I certainly am,' said Casey. 'I'll just hang me jacket in that shed over yonder.'

'That's not a shed,' said the foreman. 'That's your hod!'

'My God, 'tis a fearsome sight to be sure,' Casey gasped. 'But I can manage it if you'll help me tie a sack of cement to each of my boots so that I don't break into a run when I'm climbing the ladder.'

Off our hero duly sped with dozens of bricks in his hod, 20 feet up a ladder to the first level and then across a narrow plankway. The foreman suddenly realized that Casey was hopping along on one foot.

'Hey, why are you hopping?' he called.

'I don't think this plank will take me full weight,' cried Casey, just as the trouble started. Answering the boss's shout had made him look down, and suddenly vertigo set in.

'Begod, I'm going dizzy, sor!' he called.

'Well, come down then.'

'But how will I get down, sor?'

'The same way you went up.'

'But I came up head first,' screamed Casey, just as he slipped and fell.

Twenty feet down he dropped into a pile of sand

which broke most of his fall.

'Are you all right?' shouted the anxious foreman.

'I think so, sor,' said Casey.

'Bring him a glass of water,' ordered the foreman.

'In the name of God,' said Casey, 'how far do you have to fall to get whiskey?'

'Have you any work for me, sor?' inquired Micky Cassidy of the foreman.

'You can help that gang in the trench over there.'

Over went Cassidy to the trench and jumped in, falling 15 feet.

'Why didn't you use the ladder?' shouted the boss.

'I thought they were for going up!' cried Micky.

That tale may not be as far-fetched as it seems. Certainly as true as the saga of Pete McCarthy's first day at work. Joining the other labourers, Pete picked up the only shovel he could find.

'Don't use that shovel. If Big Jamie sees you with his shovel he'll kill you!'

So Pete looked around and grabbed the only pick he could find.

'For God's sake put down that pick,' said another 'That's Big Jamie's pick. If he sees you with that he'll kill you.'

Come tea break and Pete had done no work, but

fancied a mug of tea. Picking up the only free mug on the tray, he was warned:

'That's Big Jamie's mug. If Big Jamie sees you with that mug he'll kill you!'

'That does it,' screamed McCarthy. 'I'm sick to death of hearing about this Big Jamie. I'm going to sort him out. Where does he live?'

'Winslow Street – number 7.'

So McCarthy grabbed a shovel and marched off to Winslow Street, hammered on the door, brushed past the little old lady who opened it and stormed into the house. From an upstairs room he could hear monstrous snoring noises so up he ran and burst into the bedroom. There on a bed lay a giant, six feet four inches, at least 18 stones, covered in hair.

Without a word McCarthy laid into the beast with his shovel – crash! clang! bang!

'Merciful heavens,' screamed the little old lady. 'If Big Jamie sees you hitting the baby he'll kill you!'

Rooney was seen trying to shin up a huge flagpole, and having little success.

'What's the problem?' asked Magee.

'The boss wants me to measure this pole,' said Rooney.

'Well, to save yourself the effort why don't you lay the pole down?' Magee said.

'No good,' reasoned Rooney. 'He wants the height not the length.'

Sign on the side of an Irish van:
 Eamonn Feason. International Plumber
 Paris, Madrid, Las Vegas. But mostly Dublin.

'Have you work for a handyman?' asked Murphy.
 'Depends what you can do,' said the hotel
manager.
 'Are you good at electrics?'
 'No, sor.'
 'Plumbing?'
 'No, sor.'
 'Painting and decorating?'
 'No, sor.'
 'Carpentry?'
 'No, sor.'
 'Well what makes you say you're a handyman?'
 'I only live next door, sor!'

Of course not all Irishmen are labourers. Indeed no.
Take the wife of the Irish jockey who had been
widowed when a bus load of jockeys were killed in a
crash. She had to go to the morgue to identify her
husband. As she pulled back the covers she said:
 'That's not him!'
 'That's not him!'
 'That's not him!'
 'Typical of Murphy, never in the first three!'

When the Channel Tunnel was under consideration, a request went out for tenders for the construction. International companies sent in quotes but the lowest came from the Reilly Brothers of Sligo – total cost £150.

'How can you tender for such a low amount?' inquired the government official.

'Well,' replied Reilly, 'it's because there'll be two of us digging at the same time. One from France and one from England and we meet up in the middle.

'But,' said the government man, 'you've only got to be one centimetre out and you'll miss each other completely.'

'In that case,' said Reilly, 'you'll get two tunnels for the price of one!'

Logical isn't it?

'I'd like you to brush out the machine shop,' said the factory manager, handing Murphy a brush, and a pair of goggles.

'What are the goggles for, sor?' inquired Murphy.

'The sparks,' said the boss.

'Sure there's no need for them,' said Murphy. 'There'll be no sparks off this brush.'

'At the time of the accident you were in charge of the one-man bus?' asked the judge.

'I was indeed your honour,' replied Casey.
'Can you tell the court what happened?'
'I can't sir,' said Casey, 'because at the time I was
upstairs collecting the fares!'

Sign in a Dublin shop:
'O'Reilly's Kentucky Fried Chicken.
If Colonel Sanders had had our recipe
He'd have been a general!'

'What does your husband do?' inquired Lucy.
'Sure he works in a clock factory,' said Mary. 'He
sits at a bench making faces all day.'

Notice on a building site:
'The shovels haven't arrived, and until they do,
you'll have to lean on each other.'

'There's four of you putting these telegraph poles into
the ground, Murphy,' said the foreman. 'How come
they've all put in twenty, and you've only managed
four?'

'But sir,' reasoned Murphy, 'look how much of the poles they're leaving sticking out of the ground!'

Mickey Ryan got a job with the council emptying dustbins.

' 'Tis great work,' said he. 'A hundred pounds a week and all you can eat! But what spoils it is the foreman. He has terrible bad breath.'

Mickey, however, soon became an expert in the art of refuse collecting until at his peak he could often be seen carrying a loaded dustbin on each shoulder and another equally full under each arm. He would stroll along whistling a merry tune.

'Gosh, you are an amazing fellow,' remarked a passer-by. 'How on earth do you do that?'

' 'Tis easy, sor,' said Ryan. 'You just push your lips forward and blow.'

The Irishman on Liverpool's docks would leave the job early every lunchtime, telling his workmates, 'I'm just going for more cotton.'

When he died they wrote this epitaph on his headstone:

'Gone – but not for cotton.'

'Mr Murphy,' said the boarding house landlady, 'I wonder if you would do me a great favour and change the lightbulb in the dining room?'

'Certainly,' said Murphy. Taking the bulb in his hand he stepped on to the highly polished dining table in his hobnailed boots and proceeded to set about the task.

'Hold on,' exclaimed the startled landlady, 'I'll get a sheet of paper to go under your feet.'

'No need,' said Murphy, 'I can reach already.'

'You on the scaffolding – you're fired!' shouted the foreman from below.

'What did you say?' shouted Pat cupping his ear.

'You – get your cards – you're fired!'

'Can't hear you,' shouted Pat.

'I said you're fired,' screamed the boss.

'What?' called Pat.

'Never mind,' muttered the foreman to himself. 'I'll sack somebody else.'

'You do,' bellowed Pat, 'and I'll have the union on you!'

There was the Irish policeman in Liverpool who found a dead horse in Cazneau Street. Not being too sure how to spell Cazneau Street he dragged the beast into Lime Street.

On the subject of dead animals, there was the tale of Casey and McBride who were coming home from a Sunday lunchtime drinking session, when they stumbled over a large cadaver by the roadside.

'It's a mule,' said one.

'No, 'tis a donkey,' said the other.

'Here comes the parish priest, he'll settle the matter.'

'Father, could you help us?' asked Casey. 'Could you tell us if this is a mule or a donkey.'

'It's neither,' said the holy man. 'It's an ass. And don't leave it there. Get a shovel and bury it.'

Ten minutes later the two boys were hard at it digging up the soil when O'Shaughnessy happened along.

'What's that you're doing, lads, digging a fox hole?'

'Not according to the parish priest,' said Casey.

Rooney was the man in charge of Mullingar Station and he'd had many adventures in his working life. They do say he was the originator of the story of the level crossing gates. You know the one? Well, the English tourist entered the station and said:

'The level crossing gates are jammed. Only one's open and one's closed.'

'Well, sir,' said Rooney, 'we're half expecting a train!'

But don't let me digress when that isn't the tale I wish to tell. No, my tale involves the good old days of trains, postal services and old money.

In that dim and distant past it was a fact that the Irish rail service had different charges for different transportation of livestock. If an animal were placed in the caged-off section of the goods carriage of a train it was treated as livestock and the charge was five shillings. However, if the beast had a label round its neck and was merely shoved in with the rest of the mail, it was regarded as a parcel and the charge was only one shilling. So it happened that a greyhound was sent to Mullingar by rail and the one shilling was paid and a label stuck on its collar.

On opening the goods van, railman Rooney was knocked to the floor by the dog which leapt out of the carriage and raced off down the platform. Gasping for breath and dragging his twisted ankle, Rooney bellowed to the folk further up the platform:

'Stop that dog – it's a parcel!'

Donal O'Donnell took pride in his new job as shop assistant in Ryan's greengrocer's shop. Every customer so far was a nice person, easily served and easily pleased. Too soon young Donal started to become complacent. 'Nothing to this job,' he thought. 'Piece of cake, money for jam.'

Then it happened. In the door came Big Mick McGrath, straight from the pub and weighed down with the vino collapso. He drew himself up to his full six feet six inches and said:

'I would like to buy half a lettuce – for cash of course.'

'Oh no,' smiled O'Donnell. 'There's no chance. We never sell half lettuces, how ridiculous. Half a cucumber you can have, even half a cauliflower, but half a lettuce, no way.'

'Look,' said Big Mick, gripping young Donal by the lapels and drawing him off his feet. 'I want half a lettuce and there's two ways I can get it. One is nicely wrapped and handed to me by you. The other is over your dead body. Now what's it going to be – eh?'

'Excuse me, sir,' said Donal, 'but you see, this isn't my establishment. I'll have to nip round the back and ask the boss.'

Swiftly he dashed behind the curtain and into the back of the shop, little realizing that Big Mick was following him.

'Mr Ryan,' he said, 'there's a great big fat ugly feller outside in the shop. He's got scars all over his face and muscles in his spit. And boy, is he thick. He's asking for half a lettuce.'

Just then O'Donnell spotted Big Mick and went on quickly:

'And this nice gentleman would like the other half!'

Casey stood by his fruit stall shouting the prices to attract the customers.

'Here we go – apples five for a pound. Apples five for a pound!'

'I'll have a pound's worth,' said Kitty Kelly, and off she traipsed with the fruit.

Two minutes later she was back. 'Apples five for a

pound indeed,' she stormed. 'There's only four in the bag.'

'Of course,' said Casey, 'one had gone bad so I threw it away for you!'

Three whiskey reps were seated in the restaurant waiting to have lunch with the prime minister and assorted international statesmen.

'Right,' said the Bells' whisky rep, 'let's have a jar.' So saying he went to the bar and returned with three large Bells.

These were quickly supped and the Teachers' rep said, 'I'll get the same again.' He returned with three large Teachers and they were supped with equal speed. Finally, the Jamiesons' rep went to the bar and returned with three large Bells.

'Bells? Bells?' said the other two in chorus. 'Why didn't you buy Jamiesons?'

'Well, you see,' said the Jamieson man, 'it would hardly be polite to meet all those dignitaries smelling of strong drink!'

The Murphy boys sat outside the bank and Pat outlined the plan for the stick-up. 'Now, youse three put the masks on and leap into the bank. I'll be staying in the car. Then youse'll pull out the pistols from your trousers' pockets and tell everyone to lie on the floor and be quiet. Meantime, I'll be in the car doing the dangerous part. When everyone is lying on the floor you'll grab all the large notes and shake them into a sack. Meantime, I'll be in the car doing the dangerous bit.' .

'Hang on, hang on,' said brother Mickey. 'We're doing all the sticking up and shouting. You're in the car, but I don't understand why it's the dangerous bit.'

'Well, you see,' said Pat, 'it's dangerous 'cos the car's not taxed!'

The Maguire boys decided to buy and sell turnips and purchased a two-ton truck for the job. On the first day they bought two tons of turnips at 20p a pound and sold them at the market for the same price. At the end of the day Sean said, 'Dermott, this is ridiculous, we've sold every turnip and haven't made a penny profit!'

'Sure I know what it is,' replied Dermott, 'we need a bigger lorry!'

Times were tough. The recession had really bitten and jobs were scarce. Murphy had tried everything, manual labour, waiting on tables, window cleaning. Each job just seemed to melt away and now he was desperate. Then he noticed an ad in the evening paper. 'Help needed urgently at Whipsnade Zoo.'

'Who cares what the work is,' thought Murphy. 'I'll have a go, begod.'

'Well, Mr Murphy,' said the head keeper, 'I'll tell you the truth. We're desperately short of animals anyway, and now the gorilla has gone down with the flu. We're looking for someone to dress up in a gorilla outfit and bounce around the cage.'

'I'm your man,' said Murphy. 'I'm your man.'

So terms were agreed – £100 per week and all the bananas that Murphy could eat, and your man set off with a will.

All morning he bounded around the cage, swinging from trees, bellowing and charging at the people on the other side of the bars. But if the morning went well, the afternoon was a disaster. Having feasted on five pounds of bananas, Murphy decided to do a little bouncing up and down. Second bounce he landed on a loose floorboard and crashed through the cage bottom into a lower cage full of lions.

'My God, help me,' screamed Murphy, starting to rip off the gorilla skin.

'Shut your gob,' said the nearest lion, 'or you'll get us all the sack!'

Casey had got a job felling trees. (No, this isn't the one about the two Irishmen who saw the sign 'Tree fellers wanted' and said 'If Pat had been with us we'd have got that job'.) And he was paid by results. They gave him an electric saw and off into the forest he went. At sunset Casey returned with the other loggers and they counted their trees.

'I got ninety-eight,' said O'Brien.

'Ninety-one me,' added Quinn.

'I only got sixteen,' said Casey.

'Well, I can't understand that,' said the boss. 'Maybe your saw is defective. Pass it here.'

The boss pulled the starting rope and the saw burst into life.

'My God,' said Casey, 'what's that noise?'

The oil well had been on fire for over ten days. Nothing like it had ever been seen in Saudi Arabia. The world's experts had come, tried and failed to extinguish the blaze. Even Red Adair had had to admit defeat. What to do? Put up a reward! Yes, that was the answer.

So the emir offered twenty million dollars to anyone who could put out the fire and the world's press printed the news. For two days there were no takers and then suddenly, out of nowhere, over a huge sand hill came a jeep. Emerald green in colour, it was, bearing the logo 'Murphy's of Finglas'. Sixty, maybe seventy, miles an hour the jeep hurtled towards the flames with a dozen red-faced Irishmen hanging on for dear life. Into the centre of the maelstrom raced the vehicle spilling the men on to the burning oil. Up and down they hopped, stamping fiercely with their wellington boots until gradually, ever so gradually, the flames abated and the fire was snuffed out.

'Bravo, bravo,' bellowed the delighted emir. 'You have more than earned the twenty million dollars. Now tell me, what's the first thing you'll do with the money? Holidays, Rolls-Royces, houses, what?'

'Well,' said Murphy, 'the first thing we're going to do is get the brakes fixed on that jeep!'

It was his first day at work and Finbar was relishing it. He'd been given a huge truck to drive and he felt like king of the road. Southampton was his destination. There to pick up a load of forty tons of canned goods and return to Birmingham the same day. All went well while he was on the motorways. Nothing could be simpler with the route virtually mapped out for him. It was, though, a different matter when he came to the normal roads again. Suddenly signs were smaller and in shorter supply. Harder and harder it became to find the way until suddenly he was faced with the dread of all drivers – an unsigned T junction. Left or right? Come on, which one? Worse still, the road was quite narrow. Make a mistake and there was little chance of being able to turn back.

'Take a chance – take a right,' thought Finbar. And right he took and all went well for about two miles till he rounded a sharp bend and ran into a low bridge which seemed to have jumped out of nowhere. The lorry was firmly jammed and, to compound the problem, there in a layby stood a police patrol car seemingly waiting for the accident to happen.

Now the first sign of being in trouble with the law is

when the policemen get out of the car and hitch up their trousers. This they did and Finbar knew the game was up. 'No chance of reprieve so you might as well go for it,' said his subconscious.

'Now, sir,' leered one of the bobbies, 'having a bit of bother are we?'

'Not really, officer,' said Finbar. 'It's just that I'm delivering this bridge and I can't find the address!'

# 2

# The Irish at Home

'My wife doesn't understand me,' is a husband's plaintive cry. I always wonder who *can* understand him if the person closest to him does not, for surely we are at our best, our worst and always at most normal when we are among those who know us best. Unhappy would be the person who could not relax and be himself, and therefore condemned to live out an act for all his days.

And there's none so relaxed as the Irish among their own. When there's no outside pressure the real personality emerges. So here's to the Irish at home and funny as always.

Seen in a Dublin newspaper:

Prize crossword. Solve it and win £20,000 plus a holiday for two in Paris.

For those only playing for fun, the answers are on page 14.

'My long lost brother is returning on Sunday. I haven't seen him since he left Ireland thirty years ago,' said Mick. 'He wrote to say he'll be arriving at Shannon airport at eight in the morning.'

'If he's been away that long,' asked Sean, 'how will you recognize him?'

'I won't,' reasoned Mick. 'But he'll recognize me 'cos I've never been away at all.

What of Jim Farrell who found riches in America and sent home a newly discovered rejuvenating drug, guaranteed to take years off a person's age?

'Try a course of these, mother,' he wrote. 'I'll be home in six months – I can't wait to see the change in you.'

Six months came and went and Jim arrived at Dublin. Through the waiting throng at the airport came a stunning blonde girl pushing a pram. 'Jim, don't you recognize me? I'm your mother. I took one of the pills and look at me!'

'In the name of heaven,' said Jim, 'what's that in the pram?'

'Ach, that's your father, he took two pills!'

Idly the American tourist watched the Cork man dig and turn over the soil. Eventually he called:

'Hey, buddy, what's that you're doing?'

'I'm digging potatoes, sor.'

'Potatoes? Those small things? You call them potatoes? Back home in Iowa we have potatoes ten times that size!'

'Yes, sor. But you see. We only grow them to fit our mouths!'

As the Reagan twins sat watching TV, on screen came the Tour de France cycle race.

'Why do they do that?' asked Paul.

'Do what?' said Peter.

'Cycle for miles and miles, up hill, down dale. Month after month, day after day. Through wind, rain, snow, ice. Why do they continually torture themselves?'

'It's because,' said Peter, 'the winner gets half a million pounds.'

'Yes,' replied Paul. 'But why do the others do it?'

Sign on the coast road by a small Sligo village:

'When you can't read this sign, the road is flooded.'

'How long will it take me to walk into the village from here?' inquired the English tourist.

'No idea,' replied the Kerry farmer.

Off trudged the Englishman muttering to himself.

'Come back, sor,' called the Kerryman.

'What now?' asked the tourist.

'It'll take you about ten minutes.'

'Why didn't you tell me that in the first place?' asked the Englishman.

'Sure I didn't know how fast you walked!' smiled the farmer.

As a birthday treat Pat had taken his fiancée out for a meal at a very smart restaurant. The menu looked rather too expensive for Pat's pocket so he gradually whittled down the lady's choice to chicken and salad.

'That'll be £38 sir,' smiled the waiter.

'Thirty-eight pounds,' said Pat. 'Sure we've only had chicken and salad.'

'Yes, sir,' explained the waiter, 'but you've had chicken breasts. There's only one breast on a bird so we've had to kill two birds to serve you.'

Mumbling to himself Pat reluctantly paid the money just as his lady friend said:

'Why don't we have a cocktail? I fancy a horse's neck.'

'Well,' said Pat. 'I'll have the legs. They're not killing two horses!'

I like the story of the old priest who had come to visit a sick parishioner in a lonely farmhouse in the west of Ireland. He arrived on a freezing cold, torrentially wet day and was greeted by the farmer and his two sons.

'Come in, Father. My wife is through in the parlour. There's a roaring fire that'll warm the cockles of your heart. Finbar, bring the father a whiskey. Eugene, shake the rain off Father's umbrella and bring it into the house.'

No matter how Eugene manoeuvred the umbrella, he couldn't get it through the front door.

'Finbar, will you help me with this contraption, it's too wide to come through the lobby,' he called.

'Don't worry,' said the priest. 'I'll do it.'

So saying, he pressed the catch which released the spring and the umbrella collapsed down.

'Did you *see* that,' said Finbar with complete reverence. 'They certainly do have the power!'

'I want some six by four timber for the new barn,' said Cassidy.

'We don't call it that now,' said the DIY manager. 'Since we've gone metric you have to ask for 15.2cms by 10.16cms. And if you want any it's two pounds a foot!'

Two eighty-year-olds were watching TV.

'Pat, me darling,' said Mary. 'Would you ever do me a favour? Would you go into the kitchen and get me some ice cream out of the freezer?'

'I will,' said Pat.

'Well, shall I write it down for you?' asked Mary. 'Because your memory's not what it was.'

'Don't be stupid, woman. I can remember a simple thing like a plate of ice cream,' snorted Pat.

'Yes, but I was thinking of having a little chocolate sauce poured on it, so I'd better write it down.'

'Good God in heaven,' bawled Pat. 'I'm not stupid you know. I can remember ice cream with chocolate sauce.'

'Yes, but do you know those hundreds and
thousands decorations. I was thinking of a sprinkling
of them on top. I'd better draw a picture,' said Mary.

'You'll do no such thing,' said Pat. 'I can remember
ice cream, chocolate sauce and hundreds and
thousands. Just hang on a minute.'

Hang on Mary did, one minute, ten, twenty, forty.
Eventually Pat returned carrying a tray. On the tray
was a plate. On the plate was egg, bacon and sausage.

'See, I told you. I should have written everything
down,' said Mary.

'Why's that?' asked Pat.

'You've forgotten the toast,' she snapped.

The news had spread like wildfire round Dublin. At
the Point Theatre on Saturday there would be a very
special event. It would be the only appearance in
Ireland of the world-famous Brendini, the faith healer.
Tickets sold like hot cakes and come the evening the
theatre was packed out two hours early. The audience
sat in great expectation of the wonders to come and
many a one began to feel a little overcome by the
importance of it all.

At last the moment came and the public address
boomed out the news:

'Ladies and gentlemen, please meet and greet the
greatest living healer. The one, the only, the fabulous
Brendini!'

Lights flashed, smoke bombs exploded, fanfares

blared and out strode the man himself to a standing ovation.

'Brothers and sisters!' said the great man. 'It is a delight to be with you all, and tonight I hope to heal as many people as I can' – cheers, applause, music.

'Now, without further ado,' added Brendini, 'I would like volunteers on stage right now. Is there anyone out there with an affliction? Please let me know now.'

'Here, sir. Over here,' cried Murphy. 'I've got a badly twisted leg from where the horse kicked me. I can't stand without crutches. Can you heal me?'

'Indeed yes,' said Brendini. 'Come on up. Now, is there anyone else afflicted?'

'Y-y-y-yes, s-s-sir,' called O'Brien. 'I-I-I've g-g-got a t-t-terrible st-st-st-stammer.'

'Come on up to me,' said the great one, and O'Brien strode up.

'Now,' said Brendini, 'I want you, Mr Murphy, to go behind the screen,' and Murphy did.

'Now,' went on the great man, 'I want you to raise your eyes to the Lord and throw out your left crutch!'

Out flew the crutch, and the audience cried, 'Hallelujah!'

'Now, Murphy, raise your eyes to the Lord and throw out your right crutch!'

Out came the second crutch and the people screamed, 'Hallelujah – it's a miracle!'

'Now,' said Brendini, 'Mr O'Brien, I want you to go behind the screen, raise your eyes to the Lord and say the first thing that comes into your head.'

O'Brien walked behind the screen, and said:

'M-M-M-Murphy's f-f-fell over!'

Of course, the greatest sport known to Irish folk is
taking the mickey out of 'know it all' American
tourists. There's nothing soothes the hearts of Erin
more than bringing a Yank down a peg or two. And
isn't it great when it is done quite naturally. Take Kate
Murray the market trader. For many years she'd run
the fruit and vegetable stall in the town market and
she'd learned to have an answer for any situation.

So there she stood and eyed the big Texan who
was poking around the stall.

'Hey, what are these?' he asked.

'Apples,' said Kate.

'Apples?' laughed the Yank. 'Why, in Texas we
have apples twice that size! And what are these?'

'Those are potatoes,' snapped Kate.

'Potatoes? Why at home our potatoes are twice as
big at least,' sneered the Texan. Just then he picked
up a cauliflower, but before he could speak Kate said:

'If you're not buying sprouts, don't pick them up!'

When it came time for the child to be baptized Doolan
proudly stood by the font in St Anne's church.

'Now,' said Father Francis, 'and what are we going
to name the little one?'

'Hazel,' said Doolan, with a smile.

'Lord save us,' moaned the priest. 'All the saints in
heaven, and you're calling her after a nut!'

Father Francis it was who stubbed his toe and
stumbled whilst baptizing a child, and henceforth the
boy was known as 'Thomas oops McNally'.

The phone went in the hospital casualty department.

'Hello,' said a frantic voice. 'It's Mick Doolan here. Can you come quickly, my wife is having a baby.'

'I see,' said the receptionist. 'And is this her first child?'

'No,' said Doolan, 'this is her husband speaking.'

The Cassidy twins had bought a secondhand Mercedes car and were taking Joe O'Driscoll for a spin. As they sped down O'Connell Street, Joe said from the back seat:

'I say, boys, what's that thing sticking up on the bonnet of the car?'

Pat Cassidy, realizing he meant the Mercedes logo, decided to have some sport.

'Oh that,' he said, 'that's a target isn't it, Finbar?'

'Oh yes,' said Finbar, 'and a great target it is too!'

'Target?' said O'Driscoll. 'Target for what?'

'Well,' replied Finbar. 'It helps to line up policemen who are crossing the road on pedestrian crossings!'

'Never!' spluttered O'Driscoll.

'True,' said Pat Cassidy. 'Just wait a tick and I'll show you.'

Just then a policeman started to cross the road and Pat drove the car straight at him. At the very last second he flicked the wheel over and swerved round the constable.

'See what I mean?' he grinned. 'Good, eh?'

'No good at all,' said O'Driscoll. 'Sure if I hadn't

opened the back door we wouldn't have hit him at all!'

Two English counterfeiters had produced thousands of genuine-looking notes – £50, £20, £10 – and really they should have been happy with their lot. Much wants more, and they scrambled through the discarded notes that had not passed close scrutiny. Among the jumble they came upon a perfectly fine note – watermarked, queen's head in exactly the right place. The only trouble was that the amount shown was £18.

'Never mind,' said Brown, the bossman. 'We'll unload it when we're over in Ireland.'

And so they took the note with them and, whilst in Kerry, they entered a corner shop to dispense with it.

'Excuse me,' said Brown to shopkeeper Casey. 'Have you got change for an £18 note?'

'Indeed, sir,' said Casey. 'And would you like three sixes or two nines?'

Young O'Brien had met the lovely Colette at university in Dublin and romance blossomed and then fully bloomed. 'Twas not long before O'Brien was invited back to Mayo to meet Colette's family – the Cassidys, farmers of long standing.

As always, the family gathered in the front room, or

parlour, and father-in-law-to-be Mick Cassidy began
to hold court on the day's work at the farm.

While tea and cakes and sandwiches were brought
in, Mick said to O'Brien:

'I've shovelled fourteen and a half tons of manure
this afternoon – have another sandwich!'

With that the big Texan came over to Murphy.

'No thanks,' muttered O'Brien.

'This morning I shovelled over fifteen tons of
manure, have a custard cream.'

'No thanks,' was the weak reply.

A short time later Cassidy senior went out of the
room and the young suitor said: 'Your father's a lovely
man, but he keeps talking about manure all the time.
It's putting me off my grub. Can't you get him to say
fertilizer?'

'Listen,' said Colette, 'it's taken us years to get him
to say manure!'

Murphy was driving the horse and trap home from the
pub on a warm summer's evening. Beside him sat
Toby the labrador, great guard dog and constant
friend. Suddenly the still of the evening was rent by a
tremendous engine noise and round the tight bend in
the country lane came a huge Mercedes car doing at
least seventy miles an hour. Behind the wheel sat a
red-faced Texan who chewed a fat cigar and
drummed his fat fingers on the dashboard in time to
the ear-splitting quadrophonic car radio. Too late the
American realized he coudn't pass Murphy and the

cart on the narrow tarmac strip – too late he realized
he should have braked thirty yards ago.

Too late the Mercedes car smashed into the cart
scattering horse, dog and Murphy to various points
of the compass.

As Murphy lay in a daze bemoaning his fate, he saw
the Texan go over to the stricken horse. Realizing its
legs were broken the Yank drew out a .45 pistol and
shot the beast dead. Going over to Toby the dog, it
was obvious that its back was broken – 'bang', a
second shot rang out, ending Toby's misery.

With that the big Texan came over to Murphy.

'Hey buddy, are you all right?' he asked.

'As God is my judge,' muttered ashen-faced
Murphy, 'I've never felt better in my life!'

Brendan walked into the shop and said:

'Are the cream cakes fresh?'

'Indeed, sir,' said the shopkeeper. 'They're as fresh
as the girl of your dreams.'

'In that case,' said Brendan, 'I'll have a meat pie.'

Casey stood at the altar, feet still but the rest of his
body swaying with the drink. What a state to be in on
your wedding day.

'This man is drunk,' said Father Carey to the bride.

'I know, Father,' she replied. 'But sure he won't

come when he's sober.'

'Let's get on with it then,' muttered the priest.

Through the service they stumbled. 'Do you Pat take Kitty to your loving wife…'

'I do.'

On and on went the proceedings till it came time for Casey to say:

'And with all my worldly goods I thee endow.'

'Well,' whispered O'Keefe, 'there goes his dartboard!'

The main wedding car had been hired from Reilly's Private Hire Company. It was a strange machine.

Two tone – dirt and rust.

One previous owner – Ben Hur.

So old the log book was in Latin.

But worst of all it was extremely demanding on oil and petrol. In its time apparently it leaked that much oil that Arabs were known to have made a bid for the ground it stood on!

But petrol was worse – half a mile to a gallon at the most. So bad was it that Reilly had pulled into a self-service filling station and stood pumping gas for at least half an hour. Eventually the attendant came out and said to Reilly:

'You'll have to switch off your engine – you're catching us up!'

# 3

---

# The Irish
# in the
# Pub

What could be better on a Friday night than a stroll to a place of good humour, fellowship and relaxed banter? Yes, indeed, what place could offer more than one's local pub at the weekend? Herein you will find people from all walks of life and of all opinions. Under one roof men and women will partake of brews both alcoholic and non. They will share a smile, a song and possibly a game of pool or darts. They will trade comic stories, snippets of useless information and, in the case of the odd Celt, they will trade blows. 'Tis true what is written:

> Irish men in drink are a wonderful sight
> The big ones want to sing
> And the small ones want to fight
>
> (ANON)

Mick Flaherty had supped more Guinness than enough and had stumbled out of Quinn's bar and into the Sunday afternoon air. As his drunken eyes squinted to adjust to the light, an ambulance went by at great speed. Blue lights flashing and siren blaring, it roared up the street with Mick in full flight running after it. A hundred yards, 200, 300, almost a quarter of a mile he tracked it until suddenly, lungs and legs giving out, he fell into the gutter. Then with his very last ounce of breath he roared: 'You can keep your damned ice cream!'

Flaherty never ever learned and would seek the fruits of the grain and the grape at every chance he could. So no wonder that Friday night, the holy of holy times when the work of the week was done, found him legless as usual and happily traipsing home with Billy McGee. As they sang and shuffled along O'Connell Street they were confronted by a very large policeman.

'Now my fine fellows,' he glowered. 'Would you be telling me where you live?'

'Well,' said McGee, 'I live at no fixed abode.'

'And I,' added Flaherty, 'live in the flat above!'

Probably the world's worst combination to produce trouble is three Irishmen and drink. Two will sing, four will split into two twos, but three? Three is not enough for anything but fighting. So it was one Saturday night that three Cork men squared up to each other in a Liverpool street. (Remember the first rule of Irish law – three Cork men will form four opinions.)

There they stood in a triangular bust-up. Names were called, aspersions were cast and blows seemed inevitable. Suddenly, like the US cavalry, there appeared a van load of policemen called by a worried passer-by.

'Right boys,' shouted the sergeant, 'let's all calm down and get our heads together. For a start we'll have your names!'

Not wishing to disclose his identity, drunk number one looked around and saw a shop name.

'FW Woolworth, sir,' he said with a smile.

'Well done,' said number two glancing at another sign. 'Mark Spencer,' he cried.

Number three, the worst of all for drink, looked round and then kept up the theme with the totally unforgettable:

'Halifax Building Society!'

Casey had followed Murphy back to his flat. Drunkenly they'd stumbled the half mile from the Jolly Toper pub to celebrate Murphy's birthday.

'I've got it all organized,' said he, 'we'll have a party just you and I.'

Entering the Murphy domicile Casey spotted the living room table covered in crates of beer and bottles of whiskey, brandy and rum. On a plate on the side were two slices of bread.

'Is it a party we're having?' he asked.

'It is so!' answered Murphy.

'Well,' said Casey, 'what's all the bread for?'

A man walked into a Melbourne bar and ordered a pint of the dark liquid.

'Excuse me,' said the only other drinker. 'Is that an Irish accent I detect?'

'It is, sir. Dublin to be exact.'

'Bless my soul,' said the first. 'I'm a Dublin man

meself. Ballymun to be precise.'

'Bedad, aren't I from Ballymun meself – Carberry Street in actual fact,' remarked the second.

'Carberry Street is where I was born and raised meself, and St Joseph's was me parish church, Father Dunne the parish priest.'

'Didn't I go to nine o'clock mass every Sunday at St Joseph's. What an amazingly small world. Did you go to St Joseph's School?'

'I did. I was in Miss Slattery's class.'

'God in heaven. So was I.'

Just then the phone rang and the Aussie barman said, 'Not too busy at the moment. In fact there's just the Murphy twins here.'

Irish they were and drunk for sure and they sat in the corner of Mulligan's newly refurbished bar. Across the wall opposite was a huge mirror, fourteen feet long and stretching from floor to ceiling.

Glancing around the room Pat suddenly spotted their reflection in the mirror.

'Mick, Mick,' he whispered. 'Don't look now but there's two fellas over there the image of us!'

'In the name of God,' said Mick, spotting the reflection. 'They're wearing identical clothes and everything.'

'That does it,' said Pat. 'I'm going to buy them a drink.'

But as Pat started to rise from his seat, Mick said, 'Sit down Pat – one of them's coming over!'

'Tim, you should have been here last night,' said Liam.

'Why's that?' said the big fellow.

'Well, there was a man in this bar last night selling cigarettes for £1 a thousand.'

'Why didn't you buy me twenty?' asked Tim.

'Anyone who can guess how many ducks I have in this sack can have both of them,' said Murphy.

'Three,' said Flanagan.

'That's near enough,' said Murphy.

'I'm thinking of whitewashing the shed,' said Pat to the barman Mick McGee.

'What colour were you thinking of whitewashing it?' asked McGee.

'Well, I was thinking of whitewashing it green,' mused Pat. 'But I'm not sure if I can spare the time.'

'Why don't you let my lad do it for you,' suggested Mick. 'He'll whitewash it any colour you like. He won't charge you a penny and it'll be a few quid for the boy as well!' (Now *there's* Irish logic.)

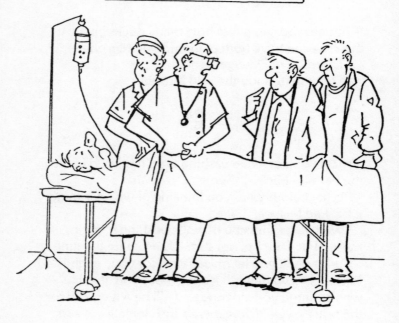

'Excuse me, landlord, but do lemons have legs?' asked O'Connor.

'I don't think so, why do you ask?'

'Well, I think I've squeezed your budgie into me gin!'

A scuffle started in the local one Friday night. Words were exchanged, then insults and finally blows. Bottles, glasses, people, flew through the air and Casey ended up being hit in the face by a sharp piece of glass which cut off his nose.

'Stick his nose back on and hold it with your hand,' ordered McGinty. 'And we'll get him to the hospital.'

Out into the street they flew to be greeted by sheets of rain pelting down.

Quickly they bundled the injured man along and into the casualty department.

'Will he live?' inquired the boys.

'Too late,' said the doctor, 'he's a goner.'

'Was it loss of blood?' asked Finbar.

'No, he drowned. You put his nose on upside down,' sighed the doc.

'Personally,' said Sean, 'I think the greatest invention was the vacuum flask. It keeps hot things hot and cold things cold, but how does it know the difference?'

'True,' said Seamus. 'But I reckon the greatest

invention is the motor car.'

'Why so?' asked Sean.

'Well, think of a summer's evening when you're out for a spin. In no time at all the windscreen and headlights are smothered in millions of moths. Bearing in mind how many vehicles are on the roads, there must be trillions of little blighters about. And if it wasn't for the motor car we'd be up to our eyelids in moths!'

'If my father, God rest him, had lived till today he'd have been dead exactly three weeks last Tuesday,' said Flynn.

'Go on,' said Dunne. 'And was it you or your father that was killed in the car crash?'

'That must have been me father,' reasoned Flynn, 'because I've never owned a car.'

'How come you're always winning money on the horses?' asked Paul.

'Well, it's all down to Saint Anthony,' said Peter McGee. 'Every morning on my way to work I pop into church, kneel in front of Saint Anthony's statue, take out the racing paper, and the holy man guides my hand down the list of runners. Never fails.'

'I'm not a Catholic,' said Paul, 'but I'd love to try it. Where is this statue?'

'Go in the front door of Sacred Heart Church and Saint Anthony is the six-foot statue on the right.'

Next morning, into church went Paul, little knowing that overnight the six-foot Saint Anthony had been removed for cleaning and in its place was a two-foot high replica.

Paul edged up to the little statue and whispered, 'I'm a friend of Pete McGee's. Has your old man left any tips for today?'

Murphy lay in hospital covered in bandages head to foot – with just two little slits for his eyes.

'What happened to you?' asked Cassidy.

'I staggered out of the pub and a lorry hit me a glancing blow and knocked me through a plate glass window.'

'Begod,' said Cassidy. 'It's a good job you were wearing those bandages or you'd have been cut to ribbons!'

'I've bought a new clock,' boasted Clancy. 'It goes eight days without winding.'

'How long does it go if you *do* wind it?' asked the barman.

It was Christmas and the mood was festive. All the world put on a happy face and joy was the norm. Well, at least for most people. Not, unfortunately, for Brendan Quinn, a man of heavy heart, and no wonder. In the scramble to enjoy every minute of holiday, he'd hit the pub at 100 mph and before knowing it, had bought the world and his wife a drink. Suddenly he realized that, Noel or not, he was skint. What made it worse was that he'd not bought the turkey and ham for the Christmas dinner. What to do? How to explain it all to darling Betty? Think quick, Quinn, think quick or die.

As if the almighty were guiding his steps, Brendan found himself outside Daley's butcher's shop and there was Daley's dog. Bing! An idea formed in Brendan's brain and quick as you like he snatched up the dog and raced off to his garden shed. Grabbing his bicycle pump, he shoved the lead into the dog's mouth, gripped its jaws tight and began pumping air. Gradually little by little the dog began to swell. When it was about half as big again as normal he carried it back to Daley the butcher.

'Is this your dog?' he demanded.

'It is,' said Daley. 'But it looks bigger.'

'It certainly is bigger,' snorted Quinn. 'Because it's eaten our Christmas turkey and ham!'

'Many apologies,' spluttered Daley. 'Please let me make it up to you. Help yourself to turkey, ham, sausages and whatever else you want.'

Off skipped Quinn – a man literally over the moon with satisfaction, to thoroughly enjoy the festive season.

It was New Year's Eve when he saw Daley again. As

he passed the butcher's he noticed the front window smashed and Daley boarding it up.

'What happened?' asked Quinn. 'Burglars? Vandals?'

'No,' answered Daley. 'The strangest thing. I had just repaired a puncture on my bicycle and I got the pump to inflate the tyre. The dog took one look at the pump and dived straight through the window!'

The drunk rang Dublin airport and inquired: 'How long does it take to fly to New York from Dublin?'

'Just a second,' said the receptionist.

'Thank you,' said the drunk and replaced the phone.

'Wasn't it tragic about my brother Michael,' moaned Kelly. 'Women and whiskey killed him.'

'Is that so?' sympathized O'Toole.

'Yes, he couldn't get either so he hung himself!'

Draining his glass, Murphy said, 'I must be off. I'm taking night school classes in Vietnamese.'

'Why so?' asked the bartender.

'Well, we've just adopted a Vietnamese baby and I want to know what it says when it grows up,' replied Murphy.

So Murphy had been greeted by the stunning news that he was to become a father for the first time. Jumping with joy, he couldn't wait to go out and celebrate with his pals. But first he must tend to the needs of his lovely wife Kate.

'Now my darling, I'm just popping along the road for a few minutes. Is there anything you'd like while I'm out?'

'Yes Pat,' said Kate. 'I'd like you to buy some snails. I just fancy cooking them in garlic butter tonight. So don't be long will you?'

'I'll be back before you know it,' promised Pat, full of good intentions.

Two hours later, bag of snails in hand, he was still propping up Mooney's bar and wetting the baby's head for the umpteenth time. Finally he decided to do the right thing and bade farewell to his pals and stumbled out into the night. Weaving from side to side, he eventually reached his house and tottered up towards the door. Sadly, in trying to get his keys out of his pocket, he dropped the bag of snails and 'crack' it split open on the step scattering snails everywhere.

The noise woke Kate who opened the bedroom window and shouted down:

'What's going on? Where have you been all this time?'

Murphy looked down at the snails, clapped his hands and said:

'Come on lads – we're nearly home!'

Mick Mulligan was a drinker, not a complete lush, but a steady toper. Pints of stout, large whiskies, he could swallow copious amounts and feel no ill effects. Except for one. Secretly Mulligan had a weakness for the worst kind – he talked in his sleep. Not a fault to have when late nights are the norm and drink is always present.

Amazingly, Mick didn't know of his failing until one fateful night he returned home the worse for wear and fell asleep as soon as he hit the pillow. All night through, midst his snores, he kept his wife awake muttering:

'Ramona, oh Ramona! Ramonaaaa!'

In the morning his wife woke him and said: 'It's time for work. And who's that Ramona you were talking about in your sleep?'

'Ramona?' said Mulligan, a little taken aback. 'Ramona? That's not a woman. That's a horse. A feller in the pub gave me a tip in the 3.30 at Haydock Races, a horse called Ramona.'

Off went Mick to work feeling really smug about the way he'd fooled the good lady. Returning home that evening Mick was greeted by the sight of his bags, all packed, standing outside the front door.

'My God,' he said to the good lady, 'what's happened?'

She replied through clenched teeth: 'The horse rang!'

It's amazing the people you meet in pubs and bars. It seems as if alcohol loosens the tongue and relaxes the brain to such an extent that eventually everything makes sense. A clear case of this was when the local hostelry had a colour TV stolen from the lounge.

'You see,' said Casey, 'it was the manager's fault – leaving it out where people could see it!'

Following logic like that, it is not impossible to believe that the following also really happened:

Standing at the bar, all alone, Jim Flynn was approached by a stranger.

'Hey there,' said the man out of the corner of his mouth, 'wanna buy a watch?'

'What's it like?' asked Flynn.

'Sh!' said the stranger. 'The fellow next to you is still wearing it!'

'Have you decided what to buy your missus for Christmas?' asked McPhee.

'Sure, she decided it for me,' answered Kelly. 'She said she wanted something with diamonds in it. So I've bought her a pack of cards!'

Have you ever had one of those nights when the drink flows freely, the clock on the pub wall stays still for ages and then suddenly whizzes round three hours in ten seconds? Well, Murphy had just experienced that very thing and was now staggering home trying to plan his entry, his excuse and his condition. Quietly, ever so gently, he eased open the front door and tiptoed into the hall. He was just in the process of removing his shoes when it happened. The cuckoo clock came to life and out popped the pesky creature cuckooing three times for three o'clock.

'What to do?' thought Murphy. Then all of a sudden – inspiration. 'I'll cuckoo another nine times and if she's awake she'll think it's only midnight!'

So that's what our hero did. It worked. No reaction from the missus. All was calm as he slipped quietly into bed.

But next morning brought a different picture. As Murphy's head thumped its way back into the world from the oblivion of the night, the bedroom door swung ominously open. There stood the good lady hands on hips – steely-eyed.

'And what time did you get in last night, dear?' she asked.

'Quite late, about midnight I think, love,' said Murphy.

'Well, when you get up I want you to have a look at that clock in the hall. Only last night, at midnight, the strangest thing happened. The clock cuckooed three times, then it coughed, belched, kicked the cat up the backside, and then cuckooed nine more times!'

# 4

## The Irishman Abroad

I suppose the phrase 'The other man's grass is always greener' applies to us all. From our very early days we thrill to stories from lands across the seas. Be they fairy tales of Arabian nights or Western adventures of cowboys and Indians, they instil in us all a desire to travel – to see the sights and hear the sounds that are not of our own nation. Truly our childhood imaginations would make gypsies of us all if they were allowed to. And nowhere is the streak of wanderlust found to be more pronounced than in the hearts of the Irish.

The Emerald Isle has given the world the best of music, drama, wit and wisdom, but its greatest export has been its people – those who designed, built, maintained, demolished or guarded the cities of other nations. Those people, too, who spread the gentle humour of Erin's Isle. So let's pay tribute to the Irishman abroad.

It was St Patrick's Day and, even though the city was New Orleans, Murphy had decided to celebrate it. He remembered starting off the pub crawl. He even remembered the first seventeen beers and whiskey chasers. But after that his brain could not recall any details. All he knew was his head ached, his tongue was just a fuzz ball, his throat throbbed and he had come to on a bed in a strange motel room. Suddenly, a rustling noise made him turn to see a very large (200lbs) black lady lying fully clad beside him. In her hair was a crumpled paper bow, and streamers

drooped over her shoulders.

'My God, who are you?' spluttered Murphy.

'I don't know honey,' she replied. 'But last night I was the Rose of Tralee!'

Murphy had been told that the streets of London were paved with gold. Newly arrived in that fair city he was ambling along enjoying the morning air when he passed a pub outside which last night's rubbish had been stored in plastic bags. One had been kicked open and all over the pavement were gold tops from beer bottles.

'Gold,' said Murphy. 'I've struck a vein!'

Hurriedly he gathered all he could stuff into his pockets and marched into the pub.

'I'll have a double whiskey,' he called to the barman, and placed a bottle top on the counter.

'This is tin,' sneered the barman.

'Thank God,' said Murphy. 'I thought it was only five – I'll have two double whiskies.'

The Rafferty brothers arrived in Britain on the Dun Laoghaire to Holyhead ferry. Disembarking, they noticed a diver clambering out of the water farther up the quay.

'My God,' said Sean. 'All the money we paid for our tickets, and that fella's walked it!'

Casey had done well at work, he'd been made acting foreman on the building site and given a big rise in pay. Naturally, he decided to share his good fortune with the folks back home in Ireland. He searched hard and long for the ideal present for mum and dad and settled on a beautiful gold-rimmed mirror for the hallway. He duly parcelled and posted it, little knowing the reaction it would arouse back home.

'Come here!' called Casey Senior, staring into the mirror. 'Mary, come and see how your son has aged since he went to that Protestant country.'

Mother leaned over father's shoulder, saw her own reflection and said:

'I'm not surprised! Look at the ugly old hag he's living with!'

'Before we enter the wilds of the Yukon,' warned the trapper, 'always remember that the deadliest creature in these parts is the Grizzly Bear. Nothing in the world can outrun a hungry Grizzly!'

'I'll remember that,' said Murphy. 'Don't you worry.'

For weeks on end the two trekked on towards the distant trading post until one morning the air was rent with an almighty roar.

'Say your prayers,' screamed the trapper. 'It's a hungry Grizzly.'

'I hear it,' called Murphy, pulling on a pair of running shoes.

'Forget the shoes,' cried the trapper. 'You can't

outrun a hungry Grizzly.'

'No, but I can outrun you,' smiled Murphy.

O'Malley retired from the British Army and got a job as an orderly in Brixton Prison hospital. On his first day he met up with an old school pal from Kilkenny.

'Mick,' said his classmate, 'I want you to keep a severe eye on the feller in bed number three.'

'Why's that?' asked O'Malley.

'Well,' said his chum, 'he's been here a month. Already he's had his tonsils removed, his adenoids removed, and his appendix removed. I'm beginning to suspect he's smuggling himself out bit by bit!'

At the other end of the justice spectrum, there was the Irishman who had been found guilty of murder and sentenced to the electric chair.

'Have you any last request?' asked the prison warden.

'Yes,' replied the prisoner. 'Would you hold my hand when I go?'

'Who's down the hold of the ship?' called the Irish foreman.

'Tom McAnearny,' replied the Liverpool docker.
'Well, one of you three come up here and give me a hand!'

'I called my son David,' said the Welshman, 'because he was born on St David's day.'
'Ay and I called my son Andrew,' added the Scot, 'because he was born on St Andrew's day.'
'Yes,' said Murphy. 'I did the same with my son Pancake!'

'Is that the *Liverpool Echo*?' said Murphy.
'It is.'
'How much would it be to put an ad in your paper?'
'Five pounds an inch,' replied the receptionist.
'Too dear!' snapped Murphy.
'Why? What are you selling?'
'A ten-foot ladder,' said the Irishman, and banged the phone down.

Answers given by Mulligan to a general knowledge test in the local paper.
Who was half man, half animal? – Buffalo Bill
Who married Adam, apple is a clue? – Granny Smith

Complete this well-known saying: One swallow
doesn't … – Make you sick
What was Gandhi's first name? – Goosey, Goosey

A workman was repairing the roof of the Liverpool
Cathedral. Into the chapel below came the widow
Cassidy bearing the world's troubles on her shoulders.

Kneeling down she poured out her heart at a great
level of decibels.

'Mother of God, help me!' she cried.

'Mother of God, help me!'

Unable to contain himself the roofer called down in
a booming voice:

'What do you want?'

'Don't be so nosy!' shouted the widow. 'It's your
mother I'm talking to!'

'I'm in a terrible fix,' moaned Clancy. 'I'm in love with
two girls and I don't know which to marry.'

'No problem,' said Murphy. 'I know you're not a
Catholic but I think the church could help you. Call in
tomorrow morning, kneel down and try a sincere
prayer to God – that should do the trick.'

Next morning Murphy arrived to find Clancy with a
beaming smile.

'It worked. It's a miracle,' he enthused. 'I walked in,

knelt down and there it was written in red across the altar cloth: AVE MARIA!'

Letter (or part thereof) from mother in Cork to son working in New York:

'Dear Paddy,

Your father has a new job, with 2,000 people under him. He's a gardener at the local cemetery.

Since I last wrote I have had all my teeth out and a new cooker put in.

I was going to send you a turkey but it got better.

I sent you a coat in the post. When the post office weighed it they said I'd have to pay extra for the buttons because they were so heavy. So I cut the buttons off. You'll find them in the top pocket.

We've had a threatening letter from the undertaker. Unless we pay the outstanding money for your grandma's funeral by Wednesday – up she comes.

I must close now. I would have enclosed some money, but I'd already sealed the envelope.

A team of council workers were drilling nearby and accidentally cut through the drains to the house. Since then there's been a terrible smell from your loving mother, Nancy.'

Seamus had a major mishap on his first day of mountain climbing. He slipped from a highish peak and fell twenty feet, stopping himself only by grabbing hold of a very, very small clump of bushes. There he hung, every second expecting the bushes to snap and send him hurtling hundreds of feet to his death.

'Is there anyone up there? Is there anyone who can help me? Is there anyone at all?'

Suddenly the heavens boomed with the sound of a mighty voice:

'I am the Almighty. I am here to help you, Seamus. Trust me. Let go of the bush and let yourself drop and I will catch you in my arms and carry you safely to earth!'

Seamus pondered for a while, and then said, 'I appreciate the offer. But is there anyone else up there?'

'What was all the crashing and banging?' asked Mulligan.

'The train ran over a cow,' said the ticket collector.

'Was it on the line?' said Mulligan.

'No, we had to chase it up the embankment but we got it eventually,' said the railman.

Reilly had joined the British Parachute Regiment and was on his first drop. Falling from the plane his chute wouldn't open. Pulling his reserve handle he realized that that chute was also useless. Plummeting towards earth, Reilly saw another person coming up towards him – it was Murphy.

'Do you know anything about parachutes?' cried Reilly.

'No,' said Murphy. 'Do you know anything about gas cookers?'

Sign in a London pub: 'Happy hour – all you can drink for £1.'

Murphy went up to the bar and said 'I'll have two quids' worth please.'

Legionnaire Molloy had become detached from the regiment and wandered aimlessly across the burning desert sand. Hour after hour, day after day, he trudged on, water all gone, almost totally dehydrated. At almost his last breath he rounded a sand dune and there stood an immaculately dressed Arab with a tray around his neck.

'Water, water, for God's sake give me water,' screamed Molloy.

'Do you want to buy a tie?' asked the Arab.

'Indeed I don't,' said Molloy, and stumbled on.

Two miles later he came across a second Arab, again immaculately dressed, a tray around the neck.

'Water, water – you must give me water!' mumbled Molloy.

'No water, effendi. But do you want to buy a tie?' said the Arab.

'I don't, I don't,' bellowed Molloy and on he stumbled.

Two miles later he couldn't believe his eyes. Mirage? No! It was for real – a beautiful hotel set in an oasis, swimming pool, golf course, tennis courts. Up the steps shuffled Molloy, calling:

'Thank God I'm saved. Water, please, water!'

Out stepped a smartly dressed doorman who said:

'I'm sorry sir, but you can't come in if you're not wearing a tie!'

'What a wonderful life,' thought Casey. 'Voted best salesman in Dublin and given a huge bonus and treated to a week's holiday at the George V Hotel in Paris. What a life!'

And so, with featherlight tread, he tripped down to breakfast the first morning and was seated across from a pleasant-faced Frenchman who stood up at Casey's approach and said, '*Bon appetit*.'

'Finbar Casey,' replied the Irishman.

Next morning, the same thing.

'*Bon appetit*,' from the Frenchman.

'Finbar Casey,' from the salesman.

However, as Casey was leaving the restaurant, a waiter decided to explain matters to him.

'You see, monsieur,' said the waiter, 'he is French

and he is wishing you *Bon appetit*, not telling you his name.'

'Understood,' said Casey. 'Tomorrow I'll put it right!'

So tomorrow dawned as tomorrows will, and Casey entered the restaurant, nodded to the Frenchman and said, '*Bon appetit!*'

Whereupon the Frenchman rose and replied: 'Finbar Casey!'

It was the maiden flight of the new Jumbo Jet 747-400. Mr and Mrs Murphy had been lucky enough to get seats aboard. There they sat, in comfortable seats, with not a care in the world, as the captain of the plane addressed the passengers on the tannoy.

'Ladies and gentlemen, welcome aboard this beautiful aeroplane. It was built by the finest technology the world has ever seen – it is a miracle of modern engineering!'

Pat Murphy smiled at Molly with pride and joy in his eyes as the pilot went on:

'On your left you can see the full-size cinema aboard. On your right is the bowling alley. Below you, downstairs, is the Olympic-size swimming pool and race track. Over your heads, one floor up, is the bar, disco and restaurant.'

Happily the Murphys began to relax, just as they heard the captain conclude by saying:

'So if you'd all like to sit back and take it easy I'll try and get this thing off the floor!'

It must be the Irish who bring out the worst in air travel. Take the case of Ryan and Rourke who were travelling to America, flying for the first time and, more than apprehensive, they were frightened stiff. Every noise, every jerk of the plane had their hearts beating fast. To make matters worse they had one of those pilots who likes to relate every little detail to the passengers.

'Ladies and gents,' he began, 'you may have noticed a wee jolt just now. That was in fact the number one engine cutting out. It's a little irregular but don't worry because we have three more. It does mean though that we'll be an hour late reaching New York.'

Hardly five minutes were gone before the man was on the microphone again:

'Apologies folks, but we've lost engine number two. We still have two left, but we will be another hour late.'

Before the tremors of panic had settled themselves, the boys heard the next fatal announcement:

'Once again, my apologies ladies and gentlemen, but it now seems that we've lost number three engine. This will delay us a further two hours.'

'Begod,' said Ryan to Rourke, 'if we lose the last engine we'll be up here all day!'

Kate McCann had decided that in order to raise a few extra pounds, or win a holiday perhaps, her husband Pat would enter a TV game show. Unfortunately, Pat's looks and personality did not lend themselves to the normal jolly type quizzes where knowledge is secondary to fun. So what to do?

'Well,' thought Kate, 'if they say he looks too serious, then let him enter a serious quiz show. And what's more serious than *Mastermind*?'

So McCann duly applied and was accepted for the highbrow show. But what to answer questions on? General knowledge? – not allowed. Drinks and drinking? – definitely not allowed.

'Pick something Irish,' prompted Kate. 'They won't know a lot of questions about that.'

So Pat decided on the Easter Rising of 1916. (They wouldn't know details from that far back!)

Came the fateful night and Magnus Magnusson called McCann to the chair.

'Your chosen subject?' he asked.

'Easter Rising of 1916, sir,' replied Pat.

'Time starts now … What was the date of the Easter Rising of 1916?'

'Pass.'

'Who led the Easter Rising of 1916?'

'Pass.'

'How many men were involved in the Easter Rising of 1916?'

'Pass.'

Suddenly an Irish voice boomed from the studio audience:

'That's right, Pat – tell them nothing!'

They'd been stranded on the island now for over two years. Three shipwrecked sailors who had been lucky to survive and had made the best of the natural resources they'd found. But now it was becoming obvious that there was no possible hope of rescue. Doomed to a lonely, monotonous existence, they sat on the beach and stared out to sea. Suddenly there was a glint in the water – yes – definitely something shining, bouncing on the waves. Yes, there it was, a bottle. Yes, a bottle. Maybe there was a message in it – it was certainly corked.

Quickly, Angus the Scot snatched it up and pulled out the cork.

There was a huge puff of smoke and out curled a genie.

'Thank you, master. You have released me from an evil curse. And to reward you I shall grant each of you a wish. What will they be?'

'Well,' said Angus, 'I'd like ten million pounds, a country estate in Scotland and a beautiful wife.'

'It shall be done,' said the genie and Angus disappeared to be re-sited in Scotland.

'As for me,' said Quentin, 'I'd also like ten million pounds, but my estate would be in lovely Hampshire with my darling Dorothy there to love me.'

'It shall be done,' said the genie again, and off went the Englishman.

'And what about you?' said the spirit to Murphy. 'What is your wish?'

'Well,' said the Kerryman, 'I don't want money or land. I'm lonely and need company. I wish the two lads were back here!'

81

Casey had decided on a holiday with a difference. No seaside this year, no holiday park, no caravan. No, this year he would go abroad. Somewhere in Europe. France? Yes, France.

'But surely you'll have terrible trouble with the language,' suggested Kelly.

'Not at all,' said Casey. 'Sure I've studied French for over two weeks and I have it off to a T.'

'Well, give me an example,' pressed Kelly, totally unconvinced.

'Well,' explained Casey, 'supposing I was lost in France and I was hungry. I would go to a farmhouse and say to the farmer: *Pardonnez moi monsieur, avez-vous un oeuf?* and he'd give me an egg.'

'That's all very well,' argued Kelly. 'But supposing you want two eggs, what then?'

'Exactly the same,' sighed Kelly. 'I would say: *Avez vous trois oeufs?* and he'd give me three and I'd give him one back!'

# 5

---

# The Irishman at War

Much as we tend to underestimate their prowess and ridicule their standing, politicians are our main buffer against international hostilities. Wars tend only to break out when diplomacy breaks down. 'Jaw jaw,' as Churchill said, 'is always better than war war.'

But when all has been tried including the government's patience, and no alternative rears its head, then fighting follows. Serious though this situation may be, it does not mean it can't be amusing as well. As many funny tales come from strife as from peacetime and, when talking about the Irish, it's the rule rather than the exception.

Two men were scuffling outside a pub when along came a huge Irishman – fists like hams – who started taking his coat off.

'You're fighting about Ireland, aren't you?' he demanded.

'No, no,' said both men in unison. 'Honestly, it's a personal matter, nothing to do with Ireland at all.'

'Huh,' muttered the Paddy, and shuffled off. Two seconds later he was back, tearing off his coat saying:

'So Ireland's not worth fighting about, eh?'

That's the Irish. Not sure what they're fighting for, but quite prepared to die for it. So here's a tribute to the Irish at war.

'We're almost out of ammunition,' shouted the soldier to Sergeant Casey.

'Don't let the enemy know,' called Casey. 'Keep firing!'

Murphy had been on the firing range for over an hour and hit nothing.

'It's no good,' he said to the corporal. 'I'll never make a soldier. I'm going off to shoot myself.'

'Take plenty of ammunition,' advised the corporal.

The two Irishmen had fought for the rebels in a South American republic. Captured by government troops they faced a firing squad.

'Is there any last word you would like to say before you're shot?' asked the captain.

'Yes,' shouted Flanagan. 'I'd like to say that your president is the biggest twit on God's earth.'

'Quiet!' snapped Murphy. 'Don't cause trouble!'

Then there was the Irish firing squad that stood in a circle!

All the recruits were giving details of their former occupations.

'In civilian life I was a jockey,' said Murphy.

'Squad shun,' said the sergeant.

'Quick march,' he ordered.

'Squad halt!' They all stopped except the Irishman, and chaos prevailed.

'Let's do that again,' muttered the sergeant.

'Quick march!'

'Squad halt – Murphy whoa!'

The two Kerrymen stood on the deck of the submarine when the order rang out:

'Dive, dive, dive.'

Off the deck they leapt into the sea, just as the sub went down.

'Begod, Paddy,' said Mick, 'we only just got off before it sank!'

Casey joined the Home Guard during the Second World War and was given a rifle, ammunition and a very important task.

'I want you to guard the town against enemy insurgents,' said the captain. 'We've got a curfew in force. Anyone out of doors after midnight is to be shot on sight!'

There stood Casey at the town square, ever alert,

when suddenly a figure came out of the darkness.

'Who goes there?' called Casey.

'Mick McGee,' came the answer.

Bang! Casey shot the man down.

'Good shot,' said the captain, 'but it's only eleven thirty.'

'Yes,' said Casey, 'but I know where he lived and he'd never have made it home in time!'

The two Irishmen were escaping from the prison camp by scaling the fence. One stumbled and the guard called, 'Who goes there?'

'Miaow!' came the reply from Pat, and away he crept.

The second stumbled and the guard again called, 'Who goes there?'

Mick answered 'Another cat!'

Cromwell's army were sweeping across Erin's Isle, crushing all before them. But they suddenly came to a grinding halt outside Cork city.

'What's the problem?' demanded Cromwell.

'It's Big Mick the Prince of Cork, he's over the hill in a cave and we can't winkle him out!'

Just then Big Mick's voice bellowed:

'Oliver. Send in your toughest man to face me!'

So in was sent a sergeant who stood 6 foot 8 inches

and weighed 200lbs, armed to the teeth with sword, knife and pistols.

Ten seconds later a great cry of anguish was heard, followed by Big Mick shouting:

'He's a pussy cat, Oliver – send in your five next toughest men!'

In rode five armour-clad Ironsides, lances, swords and guns. A terrible screaming and wailing followed and again they heard Big Mick:

'Come on, Ollie me boy – send in twenty of your toughest!'

Off rode the twenty, preceded by a salvo of cannon and a volley of musket fire. Again, a great screaming was heard followed by the sight of one Roundhead, bleeding head to foot. He crawled towards Cromwell gasping:

'Sire, don't send in any more men. It's a trap – there's two of them!'

Murphy had been caught behind the German lines and was being interrogated by the Gestapo. Outside the cell other prisoners were listening and this is what they heard.

'I want to know your name!' – Smack!

'Who you were working with!' – Smack!

'How many were in your group.' – Smack!

'And stop hitting me while I'm asking you questions!'

'Private Muldoon, you are the worst shot I've ever seen!' said the corporal.

'Does that mean I won't be going to the front?' asked Muldoon hopefully.

'No, son,' said the corporal. 'It means you won't be coming back.'

The captain called Sergeant O'Malley to his office.

'I've news about Private Morrison,' he said. 'Apparently his father has passed away. Now you know how easily he can be upset, so break the news gently, sarge.'

Out strode O'Malley and called the squad together.

'Attention!' he bawled. 'Morrison – your father's dead!'

Morrison collapsed in a heap at the news and had to be hospitalized for a fortnight.

Sometime shortly after, it came through that Morrison's mother had passed away of grief.

'Let's be careful this time, Sergeant. Try to tell him in a more subtle way.'

'Right, sir,' said O'Malley and marched out to the parade ground.

'Squad attention!' he roared.

'All those with mothers one pace forward – not you, Morrison!'

'I'm a member of the Irish Secret Service,' boasted Murphy. 'And I don't care who knows it!'

'You lot are a complete disgrace,' bellowed the sergeant major. 'That's the worst straight line I've ever seen. All fall out and come and take a look at it!'

The Quinn twins were almost identical except that Pat had one huge eye and one normal one, while Mick had one huge ear and one normal one. They both volunteered to join Walter Raleigh in his round the world voyage.

'With my big eye, sor, I can see for miles. I'd be ideal in the crow's nest look-out,' said Pat.

'Agreed,' said Raleigh.

'And with my big ear I can hear even the quietest sound,' said Mick. 'I'd be ideal on deck listening for any talk of mutiny.'

So both Quinns were hired and duly the ship set sail.

Three days out, Pat called from the crow's nest.

'Ship on the port bow.'

Raleigh took out his telescope and scanned the horizon – nothing.

'It's there, skipper, believe me,' answered Pat.

Three hours later a tiny speck could be seen through the telescope.

'My God, what amazing sight you have!'

'Yes, and she's a Portuguese man-of-war,' said Pat.

'How do you know that?' asked Raleigh. 'Surely you can't see the flag?'

'No, sor,' said Pat. 'But my brother can hear them talking.'

'Adolf Hitler drives down this road every night at 9.15 pm,' said Casey the commando. 'We'll catch him in cross-fire and blow the devil's brains out.'

'Right,' said Murphy.

'Make no mistakes. Pour in the bullets and riddle his evil carcass. Rip him to shreds,' added Casey.

'Right,' said Murphy.

'Smash him to pulp, lob grenades and phosphorous bombs and obliterate him from the face of the earth!'

'Right,' said Murphy.

There they lay, the two intrepid Kerrymen. Nine o'clock, 9.15, 9.30 – still no Hitler.

'He's awful late,' said Casey. 'I hope nothing's happened to him!'

'You've lost your rifle, Muldoon?' said the captain at Dunkirk.

'Yes, sir. In the retreat I jumped aboard a boat and the gun fell in the water!'

'Well, son, that was government property and you'll have to pay for it out of your wages.'

'What?' said Muldoon. 'Do you mean we've got to pay for any equipment we lose?'

'Of course,' said the captain. 'It's your responsibility after all.'

'And if I'd lost a tank, I'd have to pay?'

'You would.'

'My God,' muttered Muldoon. 'No wonder those captains go down with their ships!'

Mick Malone was a legend in the First World War. He was the most famous sniper in the history of warfare. The list of his victims was hundreds of names long, and yet his system was so simple. He'd worked out that ninety per cent of Germans were called Hans. So Mick would lie in no man's land, settle in a shell hole, set up the rifle and call:

'Hello, Hans, are you there?'

And a German head would rise up and shout '*Ja!*'

Whereupon Malone would shoot him.

This worked very well for many months until he came across an equally smart German sniper. This man had worked out that over fifty per cent of Irishmen were called Mick, so he tried the same plan. There he lay, directly opposite Malone, and called out:

'Are you there, Mick?'

'Yes, is that you Hans?' said Malone without moving.

The German rose up and said, '*Ja!*' and Mick shot him...

JIM HUTCHINGS.

It was no man's land in the Battle of the Somme, and a small British raiding party had left their trenches to scout the terrain. There in the mud they spotted a head, with steel helmet on, sticking out of the mud.

'Hello there,' called the lieutenant. 'Who are you?'

'I'm Corporal McGinty, sir,' came the shrill Irish voice. 'I'm a member of the 17th cavalry regiment, and I've got myself stuck in this mud and I'm sinking fast!'

'Don't worry, lad,' called the officer. 'We'll soon get you free.'

With that the soldiers looped a rope around themselves, fastened it to a tree and crawled out to lever McGinty from the mud. Muscles bulging, eyes popping, they pulled his head, his neck, his ears, anything they could grab. They heaved till his shoulders started to come free, but by now they were almost exhausted.

'Lieutenant, sir,' said McGinty, 'do you think it would help if I took me feet out of the stirrups?'

It was the height of the war and ships were being lost at a terible rate from submarine activity in the North Atlantic. It seemed that no ship lasted more than five or six trips before being torpedoed and sunk. All that is except the *Emerald Isle* freighter skippered by Seamus McKenna and crewed by Kerry's finest. The *Emerald Isle* had survived over fifty trips. Eventually news of this amazing feat was sent to the Admiralty and their lordships decided to find out the secret.

They placed a veteran officer on board and he questioned the skipper.

'We can't believe that your survival is just down to good luck,' he said.

'No, no. Not at all,' replied McKenna. 'Sure, our success is due to a very simple anti-torpedo drill. Wait till we're in the thick of it and we'll show you.'

Two days later the convoy reached the notorious stretch of sea called 'Submarine Alley'. Within twenty minutes, five ships had been hit and blown up. Suddenly, the lookout on the *Emerald Isle* called 'Torpedo on the port bow!' Out in the distance the British officer could see the bubbles and the track of the torpedo.

'Right, lads,' called McKenna. 'Torpedo drill. Everyone to the port side.'

Every man ran to the rail.

'Now,' shouted McKenna. 'Everybody lift!'

The two Kerrymen were wending their way home from the pub in London's East End. The Blitz was at its height with German bombers overhead every night.

''Tis a terrible time to be in London,' said Pat. 'With no defence against the terrible air raids.'

'Sure it was, until now,' said Mick. 'Now of course they've found the answer. That's it up in the sky – barrage balloons!'

Mick pointed to the massive inflated objects

hovering over the city on guide wires.

'You see,' he explained, 'the German planes come over and bump into the balloons and are destroyed.'

'But surely,' argued Pat, 'when the planes hit them the balloons will burst.'

'Indeed not,' said Mick. 'You see, the balloons are full of concrete.'

The Cold War was at its height when Brezhnev was in charge of Russia. Things did not look so good in the West and the mayor of Ballygobackwards was distressed.

'Inhumanity, suffering, international distrust, all because of one man and one country,' he said. ''Tis time someone took him to task.'

'Agreed,' said the rest of the council. 'Agreed!'

'Right then,' said the major. 'We'll declare war on Russia as of now and tell them that if they don't toe the line we'll invade.'

'Agreed,' said the council, and the declaration of war was drawn up. Paddy Rafferty was delegated to deliver the document personally to Brezhnev in Moscow, and off he set.

By car, by taxi, by horse, by rail, by sea and finally by air, Rafferty travelled till he got to the Kremlin.

'Brezhnev,' he said addressing the man face to face. 'It's war, and there's no turning back!'

'Wait a minute,' said Brezhnev. 'I've never even heard of Ballygobackwards. Does it have an army?'

'No,' said Rafferty, 'but we have our twelve policemen.'

'Does it have tanks, guns and planes?' asked Brezhnev.

'No, but we've lots of horses, two shotguns and a kite!' insisted the Irishman.

'What about ships?' went on the Russian leader.

'Aha, got you there,' said Rafferty. 'We've three motor boats and several kayaks!'

'But my dear fellow,' beamed Brezhnev, 'we have thousands of tanks, guns and planes. We have the greatest navy afloat. We have an army of twenty-five million men...'

'How many men?' asked Rafferty.

'Twenty-five million,' said the Russian.

'In that case,' said Rafferty, 'the war's off.'

'Are you scared?' asked Brezhnev.

'No,' replied Rafferty, 'but we've nowhere to put all the prisoners!'

The two Clancy boys had found a haversack in the captured German trench and were carrying it back to their own lines.

'What's inside it?' asked Pat.

'Three hand grenades,' said Mick.

'In the name of God – what happens if one goes off?' screamed Pat.

'Sure,' said Mick, 'we'll tell the sergeant we only found two!'

The Second World War was at its height and all the men of military service age were being called up. Casey, untypical of the Irish, did not relish this at all. He always stated that his religion was devout coward and determined to do everything he could to miss the draft. But the military police were persistent and finally tracked him down and dragged him off to Catterick Camp for training.

From the first moment of arrival Casey began acting strangely. He took to walking around the camp, pointing to things and saying: 'That's not it, that's not it, no that's not it!'

This went on day after day. 'That's not it, no that's not it!' He even gave up eating in favour of wandering round the mess hall pointing to plates, cups, chairs, tables and saying: 'That's not it, and that's not it!'

Eventually the sergeant took Casey to the MO complaining that the man appeared deranged.

'Sit down,' said the MO.

'No, that's not it!' said Casey.
'Well, lie on the couch,' said the medico.
'No, that's not it!'
'Have a cup of tea?'
'No, that's not it!'
'Cigarette?'
'That's not it!'
'A large whiskey?'
'No, that's not it!'
'Well, I'm baffled,' said the doctor. 'This is the strangest behaviour I've ever seen. You're obviously well off your chump. You're totally nuts. I'm giving you this medical discharge form.'

Casey grabbed the document, read it – 'Unfit to serve' – clutched it to his chest and said:
'This is it!'

# 6

---

# The
# Irish
# at Play

At a very early age and, irrespective of nationality, I think we are all taught that centuries-old adage – 'All work and no play makes Jack a dull boy.' (Not a word about Jill!)

We all have to have a bit of recreation, be it merely jogging to keep fit, playing an active sport like soccer or hockey or just walking briskly to stadiums and being content to watch others wear themselves out! Whatever, the advantages of a healthy attitude to sport are there to see. And in any sport or pastime, the taking part is always better than the winning. In the case of the Irish, it's also funnier.

Here are some accounts of the leisure activities of folk from the Emerald Isle.

'Listen boys,' said the football coach: 'We've got to equalize before they score or we've got no chance!'

'We're in trouble today,' said the same coach. 'Everything in our favour is against us!'

When Dublin played Down in the all-Ireland final, it was the only case in history when 30,000 people carried banners saying – 'Up Down!'

'I'm not sure about this duck hunting,' said Murphy. 'We've been here six hours and we still haven't caught one.'

'Maybe we're not throwing the dog high enough,' suggested Casey.

The same pair, some weeks later, had been told the error of their ways and returned fully equipped with shotguns, binoculars – in fact the whole shebang.

As they lay in the reeds giving blasts on the decoy duck quackers, they suddenly spotted an object in the sky above. It was a Japanese tourist taking advantage of the windy conditions to do a little hang-gliding.

Both Irishmen opened fire simultaneously, riddling the sails with shot, causing the whole contraption to fall to earth, the passenger falling free and disappearing into the river.

'Did we kill that bird?' asked Murphy.

'I don't know,' said Casey. 'But at least we got it to drop the poor Jap!'

'It looks as if it may get foggy later on,' said the match referee. 'So just to be sure, I suggest we play extra time first.'

'Agreed!' said the two team captains.

Murphy decided to find an interesting hobby. Animals appealed to him so he wrote to the local pet store.

'Dear sir,
I'm starting my own zoo and would like you to send me two mongooses …'
He looked at the spelling and thought, 'That's not right'. So he wrote: 'Send me two mongi'.
That looked even worse.
'… send me two mongeese.'
No, that was worse still.
In the end, though, sanity prevailed and he wrote:
Dear sir,
I'm starting my own zoo. Could you please send me a mongoose.
PS. And could you send me another one?

The boys had invested all their cash in a racehorse but it was the slowest thing on four legs. It lost every race by a veritable street. In fact it hardly ever broke sweat.
'It's a useless old brute,' said Sean. 'A waste of time, money and effort. We'll have to get rid of it.'
'How will we do that?' said Michael.
'The easiest way,' said Sean, 'is to leave it here and run away from it!'

Murphy couldn't resist the offer in his local paper.
'World cruise – £200 all in.'

Full of beans, he paid his fare and boarded the liner. On deck he showed his ticket and was immediately chained to an oar, along with hundreds of others. Suddenly a huge black man appeared and began banging a drum. At the same time six sturdy sailors walked amongst the oars beating people with bullwhips until they pulled their weight.

'This is a disgrace,' said Murphy, wincing with pain and exertion.

'This is the twentieth century, and slavery has been abolished. When I get home I'll complain to the United Nations. I can't believe it. And what about that fellow on the big drum?'

'Well,' said Rafferty, 'he's not as good as the bloke we had last year!'

'You know that the Americans and Russians have sent rockets to the Moon and Mars?' said Professor Muldoon. 'Well, I'm designing a rocket to go all the way to the Sun.'

'Surely the heat would be too strong,' mused O'Connor, 'and the rocket would melt?'

'No, no,' assured Muldoon, 'I'll be sending it at night!'

There were five horses in the race and Murphy had backed numbers one, two, three and four.

'What won?' he asked the bookie.

'Number 5,' was the answer.

'Do you know,' said Murphy, 'that was the one I was afraid of!'

'How much is the bus fare to Dalkey?' asked Cassidy.

'Sixty pence,' said the driver.

'I've only fifty,' said Cassidy. 'I'll run after the bus for a bit.'

Having sprinted two stops, Cassidy breathlessly asked, 'How much is it now?'

'Seventy-five pence,' said the driver. 'You're running the wrong way.'

Burke had taken his wife to the plushest restaurant to celebrate their wedding anniversary. They'd actually eaten very little but the bill came to a staggering £200.

'Why so much?' spluttered Burke. 'We only had the main course and two glasses of wine.'

'Ah. Yes, sir,' said the smart-alec waiter. 'But there were other things, nuts, apples, crisps, bread, butter.'

'But we never touched them,' protested Burke.

'No, but they were there if you'd wanted to,' sneered the waiter.

'All right,' said Burke. 'It's £200 less £195 for making advances to my wife.'

'But I never laid a finger on her!' said the waiter.

'No,' said Burke. 'But she was there if you'd wanted to!'

The boys had gone to Canada on a hunting holiday. They decided to go to the Yukon to hunt bear, but on the way they saw a road sign saying – 'Bear left' – so they abandoned the trip.

Next they went hunting deer, and were amazingly successful. The first morning they shot a huge stag and were pushing it through the forest glade.

'What are you boys doing?' inquired the ranger.

'We're taking this deer back to the car,' said Pat.

'Well, you've making heavy weather of it,' said the ranger. 'Why don't you drag it by the horns?'

'Good idea,' said Mick. So they proceeded to drag the stag for some time until Pat said, 'This is much easier, Mick, but we're getting farther from the car!'

The container truck was making a very erratic run along the highway. It would travel about two miles then stop. Out would get Murphy the driver and he would bang fiercely on the sides of the vehicle. The police patrol followed him for about six miles and then pulled him over.

'We've been watching your performance, mate, and we'd like to know what you're doing,' said the sergeant.

'Well, officer,' explained Murphy. 'This is a ten-ton truck, and in the back I have twelve tons of pigeons. So I have to keep two tons flying all the time!'

The horse box was bounding along the road at about sixty miles an hour so it wasn't long before the police decided to investigate.

'You're not breaking the law, sir, but we're surprised how fast you're going with a horse box.'

'Well, you see, officer,' said Seamus, 'I've nothing aboard. I'm off to the Leopardstown races and I'm in charge of the non-runners!'

'Are you any good at conundrums?' inquired the New York taxi driver.

'I've never heard of them,' said Cassidy.

'Well,' said the driver, 'I'll give you an example. Brothers and sisters have I none, but that man's father is my father's son who is it?'

'I don't know,' said Cassidy.

'It's me, you fool,' said the driver.

'Bedad,' said Cassidy, 'I'll try that on the boys when I get home!'

On returning to Dublin he gathered his cronies in Mulligan's bar and said, 'I'm going to test yez all on conundrum bandrums. Think about this one. Brothers and sisters have I none, but that man's father is my father's son. Who is it?'

'We don't know,' chorused the boys.

'It's a taxi driver in New York,' beamed Cassidy.

Maggie Kelly was off to Dublin to do her Christmas shopping.

'Be careful,' said Mary McGee. 'Those Dublin stores charge far more than you'd pay here in Sligo. They always double the price. So when you get there only offer them half.'

'I will,' said Maggie, and indeed she did.

'The green dress in the window,' she said. 'It's priced at £40. That's much too dear!'

'Madam,' said the salesman, 'believe me it is a very reasonable price.'

'Don't give me that,' said Maggie. 'I know your kind, you're all robbers of the worst kind – I'll give you £20 for the dress.'

'Look, madam,' said the salesman. 'I don't want a scene. If you calm down, I'll let you have the dress for £20.'

'In that case,' bellowed Maggie to a gathering crowd, 'I'll give you £10 for it.'

'Madam, please,' begged the salesman, 'I don't want to sully our reputation. If it'll make you go away you can have it for £10.'

'In that case I'll give you £5,' said Maggie.

'Madam, you're driving me nuts. To get rid of you, please take the dress for nothing.'

'In that case,' said Maggie, 'I want two!'

The Clancy twins decided to go camping for the weekend although neither had been out of the city in their lives and both were totally ignorant of the ways of the countryside. Seeking information they chatted to a farmer whose field they were about to rent.

'Could you tell us,' asked Mick, 'why that cow over there hasn't got any horns?'

'Well,' said the farmer, 'there are lots of reasons why cows don't have horns. They can be born with a crumpled horn and it has to be cut off for its own safety. It can be a specific type which has been bred to be hornless. But the real reason why that cow hasn't got any horns is because it's a horse!'

'Hello. Is that Dublin double two, double two?' asked the caller.

'Indeed no,' said Murphy. 'It's Dublin two, two, two, two.'

'I'm sorry to have troubled you,' said the caller.

'It's all right,' said Murphy. 'I had to answer the phone anyway!'

Old Brendan Boyle was a short-wave radio freak. Every evening without fail he would sit and twiddle the dials and receive the most scratchy and ear-splitting noises for his pains.

One evening as Brendan leaned towards the radio

set he felt a fierce pain in his lower back.

'My God,' he cried, 'I think I've got lumbago.'

'I don't know why you bother,' said his wife Bridget. 'You won't understand a word they say!'

Murphy had bought a made-to-measure suit. As he strode out of the tailor's shop, head high, proud as a peacock, he happened to bump into Cassidy.

'What do you think of the suit?' asked Murphy. 'It was made by Ryan, the finest tailor in Dublin.'

'It's nice,' said Cassidy. 'But don't you think the sleeves are a bit long?'

Back to the shop went Murphy and confronted Ryan about the sleeves.

'Well,' said Ryan, 'they are a touch long, but rather than mess up an otherwise perfect fit, why don't you just walk with your arms a little bent?'

Off went Murphy, light of step, arms bent a little, until he bumped into McShane.

'What do you think of the suit?' he asked. 'It was made by Ryan, the finest tailor in Dublin.'

'It's nice,' said McShane. 'But don't you think the legs are a little long?'

Back to the shop stormed Murphy, and challenged Ryan about the legs.

'Maybe they are a tad on the long side,' said Ryan. 'But rather than ruin an otherwise perfect fit, why don't you walk with your knees a little bent?'

Off set Murphy again, arms and knees bent a little and he chanced upon Casey.

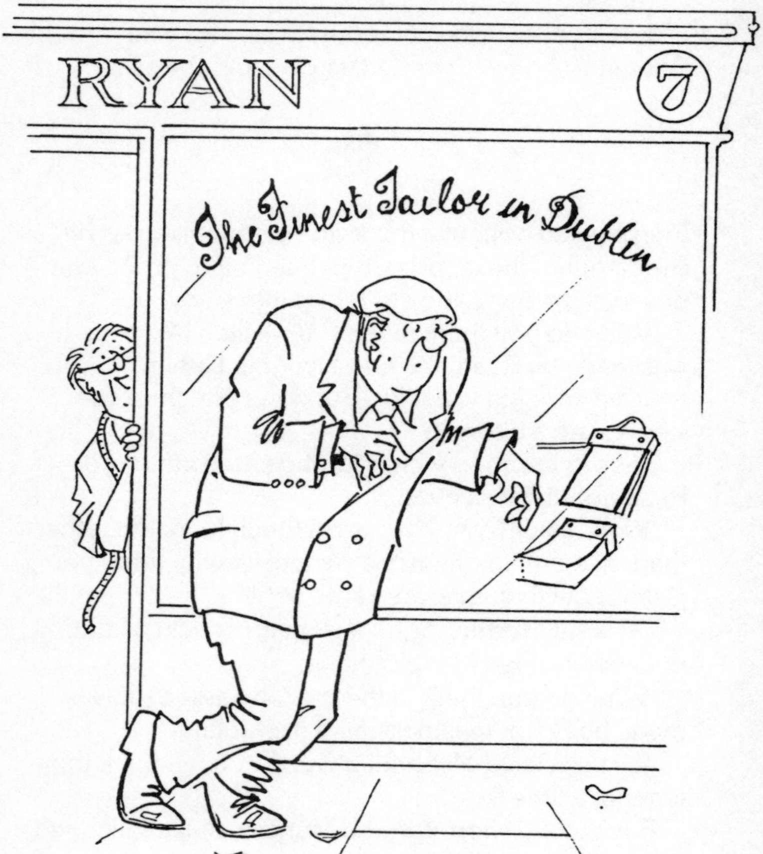
RYAN
7
The Finest Tailor in Dublin

'What do you think of the suit?' he asked. 'Made by Ryan, the finest tailor in Dublin.'

'It's nice,' said Casey. 'But the shoulders look a little large to me.'

Murphy broke into a run on his way back to the store, and snorted his annoyance about the shoulders.

'Look,' said Ryan, 'rather than ruin an otherwise perfect fit, why don't you just walk with your shoulders hunched forward?'

Once again Murphy set off, arms and knees bent and shoulders hunched forward. On his way he came upon a total stranger.

'What do you think of the suit?' he asked. 'Made by Ryan, the finest tailor in Dublin.'

'He'd have to be to fit a fellow your shape!' said the stranger.

Kate and Mick sat in the field and unpacked the picnic hamper. Out came the sandwiches, cakes, vacuum flask, plates, cutlery. During the whole unpacking procedure, Kate was troubled by an insect constantly buzzing around her face. Despite many swipes of her hand, the little blighter would not be driven away.

'In the name of God, Mick,' she squealed, 'what is it, a bee?'

'No,' said Mick. 'It's a dum dum fly. They hang around the back end of cows.'

'What?' screamed Kate. 'Are you trying to say my face is like the back end of a cow?'

'No,' said Mick. 'But you'll have to convince that fly!'

Here's a tale that not many people know. It refers to how, in one small way, the Irish had an effect on international sport.

It all began simply enough. A party of very talented soccer coaches came from London to teach the boys of Dublin the rudiments of the game. They picked out two sides of eleven each. They selected likely goalkeepers, centre backs and so on, and then they got down to the basic aims of the sport.

'The object,' said coach Jones, 'is to get this ball here, from the playing area, into that net at the other end of the field.'

'Say no more,' said Murphy and, picking up the ball, he ran with it under his arm and threw it into the goal. Jogging back he said smilingly, 'Now what do I do with it, coach?'

And coach Jones, in no uncertain terms, told him what he could do with it.

And that's how a rugby ball got its shape!

So Mooney died and went to heaven where he was greeted by the venerable gentleman at the gates.

'And who are you, my son?' asked the saint.

'Eamonn Mooney, your holiness. On earth I was a famous international soccer player,' said the would-be entrant.

'And in your life did you do anything really sinful?' said the holy one.

'Well, only once,' replied Mooney. 'It was during an international match against England at Wembley. In the last minute of the game I broke through and scored the winning goal. However, what no one knew was that I handled the ball before putting it in the net. So really I cheated.'

'Indeed no,' smiled the saint. 'Not at all. Sure that wasn't a sin only a wee wee naughty little jape – in you go – enjoy heaven, my son.'

'Thank you, Saint Peter,' said Mooney.

'No, no, son,' said the old man, 'I'm not Saint Peter. I'm Saint Patrick!'

It was England v. Ireland at Wembley. It may have been at that very match when the two Clancy brothers approached the turnstile.

'How much is it?' said Michael.

'Twenty pounds,' said the ticket seller.

'Well, I've only got one eye and so I'm only paying ten!'

And, wonder of wonders, the man let him in.

'And I'm only paying ten pounds,' said Owen Clancy.

'Hang on,' said the turnstile keeper, 'you've got two eyes!'

'Yes,' said Owen, 'but I've only come to see Ireland.'

# 7

---

# The Logic of the Irish

Sense to one person can be nonsense to another. It all depends on the way you look at things and lucky is he who can see all aspects of all the conversation all the time. For it is not always foreign languages that require interpretation. Often it is just the verbal juggling of our own language that can cause confusion.

Proof that you're never too old to learn came to me in a phone conversation with my grandson Keir, aged three.

'How are you?' I asked.

'Fine,' he answered.

'What are you doing?' I furthered.

'Talking to you!' was his reply.

Of course, I thought. What a sensible answer, and how true!

There was no questioning his logic and there was no doubting how silly I was to expect any other reply. Because, when all is boiled down, logic is merely good old nous and commonsense. Well, that is, unless you're talking about the logic of the Irish. In which case the argument can go completely out of the window!

'There's a terrible smell in this café,' said Clancy.

'Maybe it's the drains.'

'It can't be the drains,' answered Casey, 'we haven't got any!'

'I'll have fish and chips twice,' said Murphy.

'Very well,' said the shopkeeper. 'The fish won't be long.'

'Then they'd better be fat,' said Murphy.

The Clancy twins stared out across the ocean and Eamonn said:

'Look at all that water.'

'Yes,' said Pat. 'And that's only the top!'

'I'll have a pair of kippers,' said Murphy to the fishmonger.

'I'm sorry. We haven't got a pair left,' said he.

'That's all right,' said Murphy. 'Give me two odd ones, she won't know the difference!'

'Can I have an ice cream, Dad?' asked young Eugene.

'Certainly not!' said Dad. 'It's too cold for ice cream.'

'Can I have one if I put my coat on?' persisted the child.

'Why don't you give up the drinking, smoking and carousing?' said the do-gooder.

'It's too late,' replied Murphy.
'It's never too late,' assured the virtuous one.
'Well, there's no rush then,' smiled Murphy.

In Mulligan's bar, the young Salvation Army girl placed the collection box under the nose of Mick McCarthy and asked:
  'Can you spare fifty pence for God?'
  'How old are you?' asked Mick.
  'Twenty-four,' she replied.
  'Well, I'm sixty-eight, I'll see him before you do. I'll pay him meself.'

'Wake up,' said Murphy. 'The baby's crying. It wants feeding.'
  'Well, you feed it,' said his wife. 'It's your son.'
  'Yes,' spluttered Murphy. 'But he's half yours.'
  'I know,' smiled the missus. 'But it's your half that's crying!'

The Clancy brothers, lost in deepest Sahara, cut off from the rest of the legionnaires, had been crawling across the desert for hours. The heat was unbearable. The glare blinding, the water was gone and their hopes of rescue were diminishing by the second.

'Do you know,' said Peter. 'I've just remembered something.'

'What's that?' asked Paul.

'Well,' said his brother, 'today is 24 June – it's Ballybunion fair day.'

'Sure and haven't they got lovely weather for it,' said Paul.

Murphy had asked Casey for the hand of his daughter in wedlock.

'And can you support a family?' asked Casey.

'I think so,' replied Murphy.

'Well. There's six of us, you know,' said the future father-in-law.

The Maguire twins had never known the likes before. Only two hours fishing and already the boat was full to overflowing with mackerel.

'Begod, we've struck a rare spot here,' said Mick. 'We must somehow try to remember this exact location for future reference.'

'Why don't we put an 'x' on the back of the boat so we'll know it exactly?' ventured Pat.

'No good,' said his brother. 'We may not get the same boat next time!'

'Excuse me,' said Mrs McCoy to the butcher. 'But there's a sausage on the floor.'

'Don't worry,' said he, 'I've got me foot on it!'

Murphy had studied the facts carefully and had come up with the following conclusions.

The odds against being on a plane which had a bomb on board were 10,000 to 1.

However, the odds against being on a plane which had *two* bombs on board were 10,000,000 to 1.

'That settles it,' he said. 'From now on, every time I fly I'm taking a bomb with me!'

How's this for female thinking?

Two ladies on a bus and one said:

'And do you know he put his hand right up my skirt.'

And the other replied:

'Not the green one with the floral pattern?'

What about the effect of the Irish on the logic of other races?

Take for instance the holidaymaker returning to England and telling his friends:

'I couldn't believe Dublin, great city, but every Tom, Dick and Harry is called Pat!!'

(*What?* Run that by me one more time please.)

'What's that you're taking, Mick?' asked Jim McGee.
' 'Tis the secret of a good night out,' replied Mick. 'It's a mixture of Benzedrine and Valium. It makes you feel frisky but if you don't click who cares!'

'What is that statue in the square?' inquired the American.
'Well,' said Casey the guide, 'that's in remembrance of the unknown warrior – Sean McGee.'
'How can he be unknown if you know his name?' insisted the tourist.
'Well, you see,' said Casey, 'as a farmer he was world famous, but as a warrior he was unknown!'

The Casey twins had stumbled across a dead horse.
'What shall we do with it?' asked Michael.
'Let's raffle it,' said Joseph. '£2 a ticket, limited sale of 200 tickets.'
'But what happens when the winner finds out it's dead?' reasoned Michael.

'Sure, we'll give him his money back!' was the reply.

Things that only the illogical Irish would say:
'You three are a right pair if ever I saw one!'
'How come every time you ring a wrong number it's never engaged?'
'Spread out in a bunch.
And a couple for the ladies:
'Hello, Mary, how's your new false teeth?' asked Bridget.
'I'm leaving them out till I get used to them!' said Mary.
'You see my real shoe size is four,' said Vera. 'But I'm wearing sevens 'cos fours hurt!'

As the funeral procession went by, the American tourist inquired of Dublin policeman:
'Who's dead?'
'I'm not sure,' said the Gard, 'but I think it's the feller in the front car.'

As Mrs McGinty entered the house she looked up to see a ceiling 15 feet high.

'Begod,' she said to husband Seamus, 'when you said you were going to knock two rooms into one I didn't think you meant upwards!!'

The Olympic skater raced on to the ice and slipped over on his face. He recovered and then fell again, and again, and again.

Up went the marks of the judges.

Great Britain 0.0

Germany 0.0

France 0.0

Ireland 3.4

'Why the score of 3.4?' asked the other officials.

'Well,' said Judge Murphy, 'you've got to make allowances. I mean it was terrible slippy out there!'

'What does this hire purchase business mean?' asked Seamus.

'Weli,' said the sales assistant. 'To buy a TV you put £20 down and then pay nothing for six months.'

'Who's been talking about me like that?' snarled Seamus.

It was the great depression and the world's economies were in a state of shambles. Outside the small, independent Kerry Bank the crowd were gathering, all anxious about their finances.

'Tell us the facts,' shouted Jim Hanagan. 'Remember, I was one of the first people to deposit money with you!'

'Indeed you were,' said Banker Kennedy. 'And because of that you are what we call a preferential creditor.'

'A preferential creditor!' shouted Flanagan, louder than before. 'What does that mean?'

'Well,' said Kennedy. 'It means that you will be the first to know there's nothing to come!'

When it comes to paying any type of tax I suppose all races on earth combine in mutual abhorrence. But some people can handle the problem better than others, and none handle it better than the Irish. Take Jimmy Malloy:

Jimmy lived in a beautiful sixteen-bedroomed mansion out in the country. The house stood in 200 acres of prime land and included a huge garage for his three Rolls-Royces and three Mercedes limousines. His paddock saw the daily training of his string of prime racehorses and show jumpers. His indoor swimming pool was of Olympic proportions and the main house included a full-sized cinema, a disco, and gym equipped with every possible modern machine and gadget.

To his door one morning came a gentleman dressed in a sober dark grey suit and wielding a briefcase.

'Ah, Mr Malloy, I'm from the Inland Revenue and would like to ask you one or two questions about your mobile fish and chip shop.'

'What sort of questions?' challenged Malloy.

'Well, for instance,' said the taxman, 'for the last five years your annual returns have never exceeded £5,000 and a couple of times the figure was less than £3,000.'

'That's true,' replied Jimmy. 'So what's the problem?'

'Well, you see,' said the man from the Revenue, 'we can't reconcile those figures with the life you lead.'

'Oh, I see,' beamed Malloy. 'You're talking about my wealthy lifestyle and huge assets. Well let me explain. It has nothing to do with the chip shop. You see, years ago I took up landscape gardening and whilst working on a site I began digging a drainage trench. My spade suddenly struck something hard and when I revealed the obstacle it was a chest full of treasure. Gold coins, jewels, trinkets and so on. Hence my wealth!'

'What a story,' said the taxman. 'Have you any proof of this?'

'Well,' said Malloy, 'I've got this house, these cars, these horses …'

(Ah, the logic, the logic.)

'Can you fill my flask with tea please?' asked Casey of the café owner.

'Certainly sir,' was the reply.

'Good,' said the Irishman. 'In that case I'll have five cups, two without sugar and three with!!'

'Caught you!' said Policeman Muldoon. 'Poaching in the river me boy is a serious offence. I must ask you to accompay me to the station.'

Halfway out of the wood Murphy the poacher pulled up in his tracks.

'Bedad,' said he, 'haven't I left me jacket by the water's edge. I'll have to go back and get it!'

'No way,' said Muldoon. 'If I let you go back you'll run off. I've got a better idea. You wait here and I'll go back for the coat!'

'Follow the written instructions and you can't get lost in the building,' said the security man to Sean Flynn freshly up from the country and looking around a major Dublin store for the first time.

Awestruck, young Flynn made his way around the building. But, all too soon, he returned, slightly dejected, to the security man.

'Look,' said Sean, 'I've tried my best. The door marked 'Push' I pushed. The door marked 'Pull' I pulled. But when I got to the big door that said 'Lift' – I couldn't get it off the floor!'

'How did you get on today?' inquired the golf pro of Mick McCann.

'Well, to tell you the truth I didn't play my normal game – but then I never do!'

Murphy was spotted driving along the motorway at a steady speed and apparently in no trouble. Suddenly though he indicated left and pulled on to the hard shoulder. Out of the car he jumped and opened the boot. From a large bag Murphy produced a paper hat, streamers, a bottle of lemonade, two sausage rolls and a chocolate cake. Having drunk the lemonade and eaten the grub he launched into a little Irish jig. The whole proceedings lasted about ten minutes, then Murphy was back at the wheel and driving again.

Curious, the police followed him at a distance and half an hour later they saw him stop and re-run the whole procedure. This was too much for the lawmen so they decided to tackle the Irishman.

'Can we ask you the reason for all the stops and the food, drink and Irish jigs?'

'Well, officer,' explained Murphy, 'I'm on the firm's outing.'

'But there's only you here,' argued the policeman.

'I know,' said Murphy. 'I'm self-employed!'

Pat had had a bad day. Lost on the horses, no luck on the lottery, laid off from work, his lot was not a happy one. Intent on drowning his sorrows he strode in to Toolan's pub and made his way to the bar.

In front of him, lying prostrate and obviously totally comatose lay big drinking Jim McPhee.

'What do you want?' asked Mickey Toolan.

'I want to get like McPhee as soon as possible,' said Pat.

'Right,' said Toolan. And smashed him across the head with a baseball bat.

There now follows a list of inventions. They were the brainchildren of the Kerry man who was history's unluckiest producer of lemonade. Over the years he came up with 4-up, 5-up, 6-up and then stopped! And if that isn't bad enough, look at other things he produced:

An inflatable dartboard

A chocolate kettle

A soluble life-raft

A self-righting aspirin

A solar-powered torch.

O'Hanlan sat in the cafe and perused the menu. Then he called the waitress and said:

'I don't want a set-price meal, can you do separate orders?'

'Yes sir,' said the waitress. 'What would you like?'

'Well,' said O'Hanlan, 'how much is two boiled eggs?'

'Two boiled eggs is £1.50 sir,' was the reply.

'And how much is one boiled egg?' he asked.

'One boiled egg is £1, sir,' muttered the waitress impatiently.

'Well, then,' said O'Hanlan, 'I'll have the other egg!'

Murphy had won the national lottery and he was overjoyed. However, at the presentation ceremony he was greeted by a rather sour-faced official who said:

'Well done, Mr Murphy, you've won six million pounds, but I'm afraid we've a small cash-flow problem. It is impossible for us to pay you all the money at once. So what we intend to do is to give you £2 million this week, £2 million next week and £2 million the week after.'

'To hell with that,' roared Murphy, 'I can't be bothered with all the fuss. Give me my pound stake money back and forget it!'

It was an interest that Murphy had thrown himself into. Breeding chickens would have the end product of providing home-grown food and, eventually, make him rich. His fowl roamed free from the very first moment they were hatched, and Murphy checked every inch of his back garden every day waiting expectantly for his first egg.

But the fates conspired against the exiled Irishman. By sheer fluke, the first bird to lay an egg had wandered through the fence and into next-door's garden. Swiftly Murphy went round to his neighbour's house, only to find him picking up Murphy's egg.

'Excuse me, sir,' said our hero. 'But that's my egg.'

'Look, Paddy,' snorted the red-faced layabout next door. 'It may be your chicken, but according to me the egg was laid on my land. Possession being nine-tenths of the law means that it's my egg!'

'No need to fall out over it,' said Murphy. 'At home we have a simple method to prove ownership – trial by combat.'

'Sounds fine to me,' said the neighbour who was easily twice the size of the Irishman. 'What do we do?'

'Well,' explained Murphy. 'I hit you across the head with a shovel then you hit me. Whoever gives in, loses.'

'OK,' said Red Face. 'Swing away.'

Murphy picked up a huge shovel, swung it with all his might and smashed his neighbour right across the face. Teeth flew everywhere, blood poured from his face and the man went down like a sack of spuds. He was totally unconscious for over five minutes.

Finally he shivered, shuddered, gradually came round, shook his head, winced with pain and said,

'Right, now it's my turn!'

'Don't bother,' said Murphy. 'You can keep the egg!'

There they were – the pearly gates. And outside hung a notice over the left side saying: 'Men who have been dominated by their wives queue here'.

Under the notice there was a line of men stretching almost to eternity. Over the right side a notice read: 'Men who have not been dominated by their wives queue here.'

Under the notice stood Casey – all alone!

Along came Saint Peter, who said: 'Why are you standing here?'

To which Casey replied, 'The wife sent me!'

Sean couldn't believe it. Saturday morning 9.30 a.m. and there's a knock at the door and he's confronted by a debt collector.

'I've come to find out why you haven't made any payments on the double glazing you had fitted.'

'Don't ask me,' said Sean. 'Ask the salesman. Sure he said the stuff would pay for itself in six months!'

# 8

---

# The
# Things
# They Say

'It's not what you say, it's the way that you say it' – is a well-used adage. Many times, the same words spoken in a different order, or with different inflections, can have several different meanings. In Yorkshire, people use the word 'while' instead of 'until'. Hence, 'I won't be in while about Monday.' This caused confusion when a new railway crossing was erected with a sign saying, 'Don't proceed while the red light shows.' Imagine replacing 'while' with 'until' and picture the possible disasters to follow...

Now, that is only in Yorkshire. What effect do words have when applied to the land across the Irish sea. Well...

The Irish have given the world many things, including a new way of talking. No, not an actual language. Rather a different use, or abuse, of an existing one. Who was responsible for the English language must have spent centuries revolving in their graves.

It's not that the 'Irish speak' doesn't make sense. It does. But not to everyone!

I mean, what about the following:

Where were you going when I saw you coming back?

I ran after you, but when I caught up to you you'd gone.

I tapped you on the shoulder, but when you turned round it was neither of us! (Try explaining that to a Spaniard!)

Ah, the Irish, and the things they say ...

'How's your son Michael?' asked widow McHugh.

'He's at university, taking Medicine,' said Mrs Murphy proudly.

'And is it doing him any good?' said the widow.

'The dinner seems to be taking forever to cook!' moaned Casey.

'Don't blame me,' said his missus, 'I'm only followig instructions. On the box it says that the peas have to be boiled separately. I can't tell you how long it's taking!'

On another box of instructions it said 'Stand in boiling water for twenty minutes'. Mrs Casey could never manage that.

'Are the tablets doing you any good?' asked the doctor.

'Well, to be honest,' said Murphy, 'I haven't started taking them yet.'

'Why ever not?' asked the doctor.

'Well,' said Murphy, 'you told me to swallow them after a hot bath and I haven't finished swallowing the hot bath yet!'

'What a filthy place,' said Murphy. 'It's alive with dead rats.'

'Not only that,' added his brother. 'There's holes a foot high!'

At Finnegan's wake, Katy Ryan remarked about the corpse:

'Doesn't he look happy?'

'Yes,' said the widow Finnegan. 'He died in his sleep and he doesn't know he's dead yet! In fact,' she went on, 'if he wakes up in the morning the shock will kill him!'

'I don't mind dying,' said Mick McGee. 'It's just that you feel so stiff the day after!'

'What's wrong with Murphy?' asked Father Green.

'I don't know, Father. Yesterday he swallowed a spoon and he hasn't stirred since,' said Mrs Murphy.

'How far is it to the next village?' asked the American tourist.

'It's about seven miles,' guessed the farmer. 'But it's only five if you run!'

'The doctor has got me completely confused,' said Casey.

'Why?' asked his wife.

'Well, he told me to go home, drink ten pints of water and stay in bed, but I don't think me kidneys will allow it!'

Rafferty had been told to attend hospital for a minor operation, but he was afraid. So when the fateful morning arrived, he lay in bed determined not to go.

'Ring the hospital,' he said to his wife, 'and tell them I'm sick.'

'You get to hospital,' she answered. 'There's nothing wrong with you!'

So Rafferty arrived at hospital and was bathed, changed and safely tucked up in bed.

'Now,' said the nurse, 'you're to stay there and not get up. So let me know if you want a bed pan.'

'A bed pan?' roared Rafferty. 'Don't tell me we've got to do our own cooking!'

The man in the next bed to Rafferty had a kidney

removed. The next day, for lunch, they were served kidney soup.

'My God,' said he, 'they waste nothing here!'

The specialist examined our hero and said 'I'm recommending that you be given a cortisone injection.'

Rafferty rang his wife and said 'Guess what? I've impressed them that much they're giving me a car!'

'I'm the unluckiest person in the whole world,' moaned Betty McGrath. 'I bought a non-stick pan and can't get the label off.'

'She's a horrible woman,' said Murphy about his mother-in-law. 'She makes her own yoghurt. She puts a pint of milk on the table and stares at it!'

'That's my lot,' said Paddy leaving the dentist's. 'I've just had all my teeth out – never again!'

'I'd like some nails,' Mick requested of the DIY man.
 'How long would you like them?' asked the man.
 'Forever, if that's alright with you,' said Mick.

A drunken Finnegan collapsed at the party and as he
fell he caught his chin on the keyboard of the piano,
knocking him spark out. On coming round his wife
asked 'Who hit you?'
 'I don't know,' said Finnegan. 'But he had a
beautiful set of teeth!'

'God, the man is thin,' said Molly Flynn. 'He's like a
set of teeth in a suit! If a door opens and no one
comes in – that's him!'

'The baby is just like his father,' said Mary Quinn. 'But
at least he's got his health!'

The old soldier hopped in, crutch under one arm, and
called to Murphy the barman.
 'A pint of the dark stuff.'

'Too late,' said Murphy, 'we've just closed up.'

'Ah come on,' said the soldier. 'I lost my leg at Dunkirk.'

'Well, you won't find it in this pub,' said Murphy.

Murphy himself was a hero. He fought in North Africa and was a member of the long range desert group. There is a legendary story of his attempt to capture the famous German General Rommel.

After disappearing behind enemy lines for over two weeks he sent back a telegram. Decoded, it read: 'Rommel captured!'

The joy was uncontrolled at regimental headquarters. But it was dispelled when Murphy arrived back. He was battered, bleeding and bedraggled.

'We got the message "Rommel captured",' beamed the colonel.

'No, sir,' said Murphy. 'It's been wrongly decoded. It should read "Camel ruptured".'

The Casey twins were flying over the Sahara Desert when one said to the other:

'My God, look at all that sand. I wonder what they're going to build when the cement arrives?'

'What a miserable party,' said Murphy. 'The whiskey flowed like glue!'

'We're a man short,' said the foreman.
    'Well, why don't you employ me brother,' suggested Casey. 'He can do the work of two men!'
    'OK,' said the boss. 'Send him tomorrow and you're fired!'

'My husband was the hardest worker in Dublin,' said widow Clancy. 'He was the only docker with a straight hook!'

'How do you gauge the time when you're cooking the dinner? Do you use an electronic device or what?' asked the consumer researcher.
    'Not at all,' explained Kitty Carey. 'It's simpler than that. In the oven I put a big piece of meat and a little one. When the little one's burned the big one's ready!'

The two O'Briens stood on the Mall in London, among thousands of flag-waving people. Not being sure what was going on, they asked a bystander.

'Is there something special happening?'

'Indeed,' remarked the man. 'It's a royal wedding.'

Just then there was a fanfare of trumpets from the gates of Buckingham Palace.

'What's that?' said Pat O'Brien.

'That's Her Majesty the Queen,' said the bystander.

'By God,' said Pat. 'She can play that trumpet!'

It's not always the things they *say* that distinguishes the Irish. Often, it's the things they write. Like the letter from a parent to the schoolteacher explaining her son's absence:

'Johnny couldn't come today because he hasn't been. I've given him something to make him go. And as soon as he's been, he'll come.

'Or the note on the windscreen of a badly crumpled up car:

Dear sir,

I'm the driver of the truck that has just reversed into your car. At the moment there is a large crowd around me. They think I'm leaving my name and address. But I'm not. (Unsigned!)

The very stout lady staggered up the three flights of extremely steep stairs and into to the headmaster's office. Puffing and panting she explained, 'I've come to tell you why my son is not at school. He's got diarrhoea.'

'Why didn't you send a note?' said the head.

'If I could have spelt it, I would have,' she replied.

The family sat at table for the Christmas meal. Parcels opened, presents exchanged, they were now good and ready for the turkey and roast. As they tucked in, young Michael turned up his nose.

'Dad,' said he, 'this turkey tastes funny. And has anyone seen Harry my rabbit?'

This remark was greeted with silence.

'I'm just saying,' he went on, 'this turkey tastes funny and has anyone seen Harry my rabbit?'

Again silence.

'Dad,' said Michael mournfully, 'we're not eating Harry are we?'

'Indeed we're not,' assured the father. 'We're eating a duck. And it was a naughty duck – it ate Harry!'

'What would you be if you weren't Irish?' asked the barman.

'Ashamed!' said Murphy.

Supposedly true item read out during a radio broadcast:

'There was a terrible accident in the Irish Sea today. A ship carrying a cargo of red paint collided with a ship carrying a cargo of blue paint. Both crews have been marooned!'

'I was going to give him a nasty look but he already had one!'

Mary Kelly made a phone call to the council complaining:

'Our toilet seat is broken in half, and is now in three pieces. Can you tell me where I stand?'

Murphy was even funnier in writing to the council:

'I am writing on behalf of my sink which is running away from the wall!'

Brady didn't like school and school didn't seem to like him. He was a slow thinker and a very slow learner.

He always said it took him three years to get a tick. Apparently he was the only child in St Bridget's to actually fail in milk!

But it wasn't just school that showed up Brady's lack of nous, it was also the things he said. He and six pals sat in the corner of the pub and the barmaid was asked to bring pints all round. She approached the seven, with six glasses on a tray, and Brady said:

'Whenever there's a pint missing I always get it! I'm the world's unluckiest man. If it was raining soup I'd be standing here with a fork in me hand.'

'You really are unlucky,' said the barmaid. 'What's your name?'

'Oh God, you've caught me on the hop there,' said Brady, scratching his head.

'Concentrate,' said the girl.

'No,' muttered Brady. 'It's longer than that!'

An Irish proposal:

'Would you like to be buried with my people?'

'How are you, Rosie?' asked Betty McCann.

'Sure I'm in a terrible state, Betty,' was the reply. 'I'm in such pain I can't lift me arms above me head, and it's the same with me legs!'

'How would you describe your wife?' asked O'Toole.

'Well,' said Murphy, 'I would say she was an angel.'

'You mean beautiful?' said O'Toole.

'No,' replied Murphy, 'I mean she's always up in the air harping on about something!'

'I hear that O'Shaughnessy has gone all moral and virtuous,' said Pat.

'Go on!' declared Mick. 'How so?'

'Well, he's given up smoking, drinking and going out on the razzle,' explained Pat.

'Sure it'll do him no good,' said Mick. 'In thirty years' time he'll be lying in bed dying of nothing.'

The recession had hit hard and things were not good for Liam Flynn. He'd hung on to his job but the overtime had dropped to nothing and he was really scratching along. Unfortunately he'd incurred a huge HP burden during the good times, and now found it impossible to keep up all the payments. He'd had demands, red letters, threats, even writs, and for months he'd ridden the storm. But now it was getting too difficult to cope, and naturally that's when the Irish rise above all adversity. First he got a letter stating:

'If no payment is made within the next seven days, we are coming to take away your TV, your video, your dining suite, your microwave, your sound system, your washing machine and your bedroom suite. What would your neighbours think of that?'

Liam replied, 'I've had a word with the neighbours and they think it would be a lousy trick!'

Next he got a letter saying:

'This letter is a threat of legal action against you and your estate. Unless you make some form of payment *immediately*, we will apply for a warrant to enter your premises forthwith and remove property at will.'

This time Liam wrote:

'Look, friend. I have many bills and few pounds. It is impossible for me to pay every one, every month, so to be fair to all, I place all the bills in a hat, shuffle them up, and draw out four which I then pay. If you don't stop this ceaseless threatening, then next month I won't even put your invoice in the hat!'

You know those wise old sayings that have been handed down from generation to generation?

'Too many cooks …'

'A stitch in time …'

'Absence makes the heart …'

I think my favourite has to be:

'Whenever there's nothing else to say – someone always says it!'

Seems to me though it should read ' … an *Irishman* always says it,' because if the sons of Erin have one gift above all it is the ability to say a word so final that even 'Amen' can't follow it.

Here are some instances of the Irish having a word, and an answer for everything.

Murphy had made a success of his life. He'd emigrated to America, joined the Cavalry and had risen to the rank of sergeant. With any other regiment he'd have been set for life. Unfortunately, his outfit was the 7th Cavalry and one bright morning he found himself in the middle of the battle of Little Big Horn. Thousands of Indians surrounded him, Custer and the others were dead, and Murphy began to pray.

'Can anyone up there help me?' he begged as the Indians moved in on him.

From his saddle bag popped a leprechaun all dressed in green.

'I'll help you, Sergeant Murphy,' said the wee man, 'but you may not like the problem I set you.'

'Whatever it is I'll take it,' said the sergeant frantically.

'Well,' said the leprechaun, 'I'll give you anything you want, rifles, pistols, horses, ammunition. But here's the problem: whatever you ask for, the Indians will each get two of.'

'Easy,' said Murphy with hardly a second to think. 'I'll have a glass eye!'

The scene was a courtroom in Dublin at the height of the summer with a major fair in full swing and happiness abounding. In the dock stood Casey, beetroot nose and breath like kerosene.

'With what is this man charged?' asked the judge.

'He was caught red-handed, your honour, picking the pockets of the farmers at the fair,' said the policeman.

'How do you plead?' asked the judge.

'Guilty,' said Casey sullenly.

'Well, 'tis a heinous crime which you have committed,' said his honour, 'and you are fined £50 to be paid immediately.'

'Excuse me, your honour,' said the policeman, 'but he only has £10 on him.'

'Very well,' said the judge. 'Put him back in the crowd until he makes the money up!'

So the British army were desperate for men. The Second World War was at its height and the call to arms went out. First to volunteer was Big Tim O'Toole from County Wexford, a man of keen eye and acres of street wisdom.

'Would you like to join the tank corps, O'Toole?' asked the recruiting sergeant. 'We've room for a few more.'

'If it's all right with you,' replied Tim, 'I'd rather be a foot soldier.'

'You mean you'd rather slog around in mud up hill, down dale, when you could be riding around armour clad, living in style? In God's name, why?'

'It's simple,' said O'Toole. 'When the bugle blows retreat I don't want to be hampered by machinery!'

So O'Toole joined the infantry and was soon attached to HQ and eventually enrolled as the colonel's batman. He spent three happy years tending to the officer's needs and at the end of the war it came time to part.

'What will you do when you return to civvy street, sir?' he asked the colonel.

'Music,' said the officer. 'Before the war I was a concert pianist, my wife is a cellist, my daughter is a flautist and my son plays the piccolo. Why don't you come round one night and we'll give you a little recital? And what will you do when you return home, O'Toole?'

'Well, sir,' said the Wexford man, 'before the war I was a professional boxer, my wife is a lady wrestler, my daughter has a black belt in judo and my son is a seventh dan in karate. Why don't you come round one evening and we'll give you a good hiding!'

Murphy wouldn't work. The last job he'd had was school milk monitor. He tried every trick in the book. When he left school he joined every union so he'd always be on strike. Lately he'd taken to being

permanently ill. His doctor was at least a little involved
in the plot, until one day:

'Look here, Murphy,' said the medico, 'I've given
you every complaint known to medical science.
You've had trench foot, mustard-gas poisoning,
morning sickness. I can't think of anything else.'

'Just put anything down,' said Murphy. 'The DSS
don't look that closely.'

So in the space where it said 'Illness' the doctor just
drew a line.

Back at the DSS office the clerk looked at the sick
note and said:

'It doesn't say here what's wrong with you.'

'It does so,' said Murphy, pointing at the line. 'I've
had a stroke!'

So the Cronin twins went to darkest Africa on safari.
Big game hunting was their aim and catching lions
was their dream.

'Let's build a lion trap,' said Pat. 'We'll dig a trench
twelve feet deep, cover it with a net and lure the
beasts into falling into it.'

So they dug with a will and the trap was nearly
complete. Mick climbed out to dust himself down and
was confronted by the fiercest lion you've ever seen.
Teeth bared, it let out a mighty roar and leapt at Mick
Cronin. Mick ducked and the beast soared over his
body and into the pit.

Just as Pat screamed in terror, Mick called down the
trench:

'There you are, Pat. That's number one. You skin that while I find another!'

Seamus Cohen, the Russian Jew with Irish ancestors, was leaving Russia. Having been expelled by the Brezhnev regime he was being searched at Moscow airport by the KGB. In his bag they found a bust, recently painted by the looks of it.

'What is this?' asked the secret service man.

'What? What? This is not a what, it's a who. It's a bust of our dear departed leader Lenin, the greatest man of all time. I'm taking it to Ireland to be part of a shrine to the man.'

Suitably impressed the KGB let him leave but it wasn't long before he was being asked similar questions as he tried to pass customs at Dublin airport.

'What is this?' they asked.

'What? What? This is not a what, it's a who. It's Lenin, the most evil man in the history of the world. I'm going to place it in my bedroom in my son's house to remind me of all the anguish I suffered in Russia, and how fortunate I am to live here in beautiful Erin.'

Satisfied, the immigration officials allowed Cohen entry and he straightaway made tracks for his son's home in Kildare. Unpacking his bags he brought out the bust of Lenin.

'Who's that?' asked son Michael.

'Who? Who? That's not a who, it's a what,' said Cohen. 'And I'll tell you what that is. Four kilos of platinum, that's what that is, son!'

It was a great day for Dublin. The West Indies cricket team had agreed to play an exhibition match against a select XI made up of sportsmen from all over Ireland. The setting was Lansdown Road, the weather was beautiful, a packed crowd breathlessly waited for the first ball to be bowled. And then the news came like a bombshell. O'Hanlan, the great batsman, had been involved in a car crash en route to the ground and had broken his leg.

What to do? Who to replace him? Where could they turn? Suddenly – inspiration! Dillon the tinker, the greatest all-round sportsman in Irish history. Dillon would play. Quickly they rang him and just as quickly he declined.

'My legs have gone,' said he. 'I'd be no use to yez. But I tell you what. I've a horse that could do the job.'

'A horse!' exclaimed the captain. 'A horse! The man's gone mad!'

'Nevertheless,' said Casey the wicketkeeper, 'we are desperate.'

In a trice Dillon arrived with the ugliest old grey horse you've ever seen.

'Can he field?' asked the captain.

'Field?' exclaimed Dillon. 'He's the greatest slip fielder in the world.'

The horse was put at first slip and he caught out six players off the first six balls bowled. Leaping here, leaping there.

'Can he bowl?' asked the skipper eagerly.

'Bowl?' smiled Dillon. 'He's the greatest fast bowler you ever seen. Put the ball in his hoof.'

Whack, whack, whack, whack. Down went the stumps, four times off the horse's first four balls. West

Indies all out for nought. A miracle – nothing less.

'Can the horse bat?' asked the captain expectantly.

'Bat? Bat?' beamed Dillon. 'He bats like the second coming of Don Bradman.'

So the horse was padded and gloved, a cap placed between his ears and held down with sellotape and out it strode to the wicket. Down came the first ball. Crrrack! The ball left the bat like a bullet.

'Run!' shouted the skipper. 'Run! Run!'

'Don't be stupid,' said Dillon. 'If he could run he'd be at Leopardstown!'

Joe O'Reilly very seldom had the last word when it came to arguing with the wife. But tonight was different. Tonight he couldn't lose for winning. Tonight he'd come home early and made his way up to the bedroom. There lay his good lady Kate, arrayed in the slinkiest nightie he'd ever seen.

'Hello me darling,' said she. 'And haven't I dressed up to surprise ye?'

O'Reilly said nothing but went into the bathroom, returning with a straight razor which he proceeded to sharpen on a strop.

Anxiously Katy asked, 'What are you doing Joseph with that fearsome razor?'

'Well,' said Joe with a sneer, 'there's a pair of boots under your bed. Now, if they've got no feet in them, I'm going to have a shave!'

So Molloy rang up the police station and inquired:

'I believe you've caught the burglar who broke into our house last night?'

'Indeed we have,' said the desk sergeant.

'Well,' said Molloy, 'could you ask him how he got in without waking the wife?'

Not only do the Irish have the answer to everything, but a special breed of Irish folk, those from Kerry, go even further. They're renowned, I'm told, for answering every question with another question, like:

'Is this the way into town?' – 'Are you going shopping then?'

'Is this Saint Anthony's church?' – 'Are you going to Mass?'

A well-educated, but unsuspecting Englishman decided to find a question that could not be answered with a question. He spotted Mickey Reid on the steps of the post office and asked: 'Am I right in thinking that this is the post office?'

'And is it a letter you'll be posting?' asked Mickey.

Inside the perimeter fence of the lunatic asylum sat Marty Mullen, lazily painting the railings a bright blue. As he stroked the brush gently up and down he was approached by a passing American tourist.

'Are you an inmate of this place?' he inquired.

'Well, yes and no,' said Marty. 'You see I masterminded the greatest train robbery in Ireland's history. Seventeen million pounds we took. I was arrested but tricked the court into thinking I was nuts, and they put me in here.'

'Well, what happened to the money?' asked the American.

'Sure that's the greatest part of the whole affair. I managed to plant it not a mile from here. At Beckett's crossroads there's a tall oak tree and I dug down twelve feet and buried the cash on the north side,' said Marty with a smile.

The tourist could hardly stop from breaking into a

gallop as he covered the mile to Beckett's crossing.
He bought a spade at the general store and, finding
the oak tree, he dug for dear life, ten feet, twelve feet,
fifteen feet, twenty feet – nothing! A big fat zero.

Back to the nuthouse he raced and there sat
Mullen, still painting.

'There's no money under that tree!' bellowed the
American. 'No money at all.'

'You've dug down and searched have you?' asked
Marty.

'Yes,' muttered the Yank.

Marty beamed and said, 'Grab a brush!'

'The Arabs have had it too easy for too long,' thought
Professor Moriarty. 'It's time to break their strangle-
hold on the world's oil markets.'

So it was that he set out, assisted by the finest brains
in Ireland to find a different source for oil and
petroleum spirit.

One year, two years, five years, ten, they
experimented, failed, started again. Hope was
followed by despair, despair followed by renewed
hope.

Eventually, fifteen years after he began his quest,
the end was in sight. The holy grail lay before him. In
fact it had been there all the time waiting to be
discovered.

'I've cracked the oil problem,' he announced to the
eagerly awaiting press of the world.

'I've managed to produce top grade oil at little or

no cost. It comes from mixing pure tap water with camel dung!'

'What a pity,' muttered Peter McPhee. 'And guess who owns all the camels!'

# 9

# The Irish and the Clergy

From the days of St Patrick up to today, religion has been as vital to the Irish as the shamrock itself. Lessons learned at mother's knee always include the three basic themes of 'today, tomorrow and hereafter' and, while the greater good and the love of God are much to be lauded, they do leave the way open for humour. Because the clergy and the laity are so close they can easily become figures of fun.

You only have to visit an Irish town to realize how close religion is to the people. Wherever you see a church you'll see a pub, and probably a betting shop. Since time began the clergy have had a great effect, both serious and light-hearted, on the folk of Erin's green isle.

Here, by accident and design, are some instances of the relationship between the Irish and the clergy.

'Honestly Father,' said Biddie McGrath. 'Your sermons are a wonder to behold. Sure we didn't know what sin was till you came to the parish!'

Murphy rushed along the corridor of the train, opening every compartment door and asking:

'Is there a priest or a vicar here?'

After four attempts he came to a compartment where a man said:

'I'm a rabbi if that's any good.'

'No,' said Murphy. 'I'm looking for a corkscrew!'

Then of course there was the ecumenical fishing party who rowed out into the lake and proceeded to cast their lines. After a short time it became apparent that the boat had sprung a leak.

'Let's walk to the shore,' said Father McGee, as he strode across the water.

'I'm with you,' said Reverend Smith the vicar, walking behind him.

Out of the boat stepped Rabbi Cohen and immediately sank, spluttering into the lake.

'Do you think,' said the vicar, 'we should have told him about the stepping stones?'

With a glint in his eye, Father McGee said 'What stepping stones?'

Next day the laugh was on Father McGee. He walked into the church and spotted a man sitting cross-legged on the altar.

'My son,' said the holy man, 'what are you doing? Who are you?'

'I'm God,' said the stranger.

'Pardon?'

'I'm God,' he repeated. 'This is my house!'

Father McGee ran into the presbytery and, in total panic, rang the archbishop.

'Your reverence,' said he, 'I hate to trouble you, but there's a man sat on me altar who claims he's God. What'll I do?'

'Take no chances,' said the archbishop. 'Get back in the church and look busy!'

The preacher, a Jesuit no less, stood in the pulpit, high above the congregation and ranted and raved about sin, damnation and kingdom come. For twenty minutes he roared out a tirade, whilst pounding the pulpit with both hands.

Eventually young Eugene O'Malley, five years old, turned to his mother and said: 'Mum, whatever shall we do if he gets out of there?'

It was preaching each Sunday that made Father Brown a few pounds extra on the side. You see he had a weekly bet with the altar boy that he could improvise a sermon on any subject at a moment's notice. Each week the altar boy left a note on the lectern, and each week the priest ad-libbed his way through. Finally the youngster thought he had the priest stone cold by leaving a note that merely said: 'Constipation'.

Totally unconcerned, Father Brown glanced at the paper looked up and began:

'And Moses, taking the tablets, went up into the mountain …'

Father Brown was a man for the horses and attended every meeting at the local course. He got to know jockeys, trainers and officials and was a regular visitor to the 'business end' of the racing scene.

One day, whilst breezing round the training area he came upon trainer Murphy who was giving sugar lumps to the outsider.

'I hope that's not dope you're giving the poor beast?' said the priest jokingly.

'Indeed not, Father,' said Murphy. ' 'Tis only sugar. Here, swallow a cube and I will as well.'

Satisfied, the priest wandered on as Murphy dialled a number on his mobile phone and said:

'Mick, it's all set. The horse has had the treatment and he'll go like the wind. In fact if anything passes it, it will be me or Father Brown!'

Father Flynn had been parish priest at St Monica's for over fifteen years and boasted that he knew all his parishioners by the sound of their voices. So he was a little miffed when he was hearing confessions one Saturday morning and realized there was a person talking whose voice he couldn't place.

'Are you a stranger here?' asked the priest through the confessional screen.

'Yes, Father,' said the voice. 'I'm touring with the circus that came into town yesterday.'

'I see,' said the priest. 'And what do you do in the circus?'

'I'm an acrobat,' said the stranger.

'Bedad, I'd like to see you work,' said Father Flynn, 'but I'll be too busy to come to the show.'

'No problem,' said the acrobat. 'I can do a few things now if you have the time.'

Out came the priest from the confessional box and he sat in a pew watching the circus performer do handstands, flick flacks, somersaults and multifarious contortions.

As this was going on, Biddie Murphy rushed out of church saying to herself:

'If that's the sort of penance he's giving, I'm going to change me underwear!'

The American tourist was walking around the cathedral admiring the architecture.

'Are you enjoying your visit to Ireland?' asked a young priest.

'Very much, Father, but I can't get on with the whiskey – it's far too strong for me,' said the Yank.

'Why so?' asked the priest.

'Well, I got drunk on it on Saturday night and crashed out unconscious. Sunday morning I woke at 5 a.m. bright as a button. I went to 6 o'clock mass, 7 o'clock mass, 8 o'clock, nine, ten and eleven o'clock mass. Then I went to afternoon Rosary, sermon, Stations of the Cross and Benediction!'

'So what's wrong with that?' asked the priest.

'I'm a Protestant!' said the tourist.

'I'm sorry to trouble you, Father,' said Reverend Mother. 'But I'm afraid I have a complaint to make.'

'What's that?' asked the parish priest.

'Well, Father, it's the youngsters attending the Friday night dance,' explained the nun. 'When they're coming home they pass the convent and they make such a noise. Last night I couldn't sleep for the noise.'

'Do you know,' said Father Kelly, 'I had the same trouble meself. And really there's no excuse for behaviour that rowdy. Wait till Sunday. I'll give it to them in the sermon.'

Sunday morning came and nine o'clock mass saw the Reverend Father, red-faced, up in the pulpit, bellowing at full volume. 'Now the boys and girls who attend the Friday night dance. Youse are making far too much noise. Last Friday me and Reverend Mother couldn't get a wink of sleep!'

There followed the complete collapse of the congregation in laughter.

The convent had been presented with a new car, a red Mini Metro, the pride of its breed. Sister Lucy, the only qualified driver, became the chauffeur for all and sundry. Every Saturday she would drive Reverend Mother into town for the shopping.

All went well till Bank Holiday weekend when the town was so packed with people and cars that it became evident that there was no earthly place to park.

'Don't worry, Mother,' said Sister Lucy. 'You go into the supermarket and I'll drive round the block until you come out.'

Off sped the car, and Reverend Mother bustled round the store quickly, picking up all the necessary goods and then rushing back to the kerbside. There she stood for five minutes, ten, fifteen, twenty. No sign of Sister Lucy. Where could she be?

Eventually Reverend Mother approached a patrolling policeman.

'Excuse me, officer,' said she, 'have you seen a nun in a red Mini?'

'No,' replied the copper, 'but these days nothing would surprise me!'

So it was that Murphy approached Mulligan's bar. On the step outside he was accosted by a nun, Sister Marie, who said:

'Surely a fine man like yourself is not going into this den of iniquity? Surely you're not going to waste your hard-earned cash on the devil's brew. Why don't you go home and feed and clothe your wife and children?'

'Hang on, Sisters,' spluttered Murphy. 'How can you condemn alcohol out of hand? Surely it's wrong to form such a rash judgement when you've never tasted the stuff?'

'Very well,' said Sister Marie. 'I'll taste it just to prove my point. Obviously I can't go into the pub, so why don't you bring me some gin. Oh, and just to camouflage my intent, maybe you should bring it in a cup not a glass!'

'OK,' said Murphy and into the bar he breezed.

'I'll have a large gin,' he said to the barman. 'And

can you put it in a cup?'

'My God,' said the barman, 'that nun's not outside again is she?'

Although nuns and drink do not usually go together, there was another story of the two Sisters of Charity (remember those huge head-dresses they used to wear?) who were walking past the local hostelry. Suddenly out on to the pavement stumbled Mickey Kelly. Drunkenly he staggered forward towards the holy ladies. He got to within four feet of them when the nuns parted and let him pass between them.

'My God, Sisters,' said Kelly, totally confused. 'How did you do that?'

The man was immaculately dressed. Kitted out more for the Ritz than the street. But in the street he lay dressed in black tail suit, patent leather shoes, top hat and bow tie, and very dead.

'How did he get here?' asked patrolman Muldoon.

'He threw himself off the roof,' said a bystander.

'Does anyone know the man?' said Muldoon.

'I do,' said Barrie Quinn.

'What religion is he?' asked the policeman. 'Catholic, Protestant, Jewish, Muslim?'

'None at all,' said Quinn. 'He's an atheist!'

'What a shame,' said Muldoon. 'All dressed up and nowhere to go!'

So Father Murphy was making his usual Friday night calls on various houses in his parish. He genuinely worried about the religious affairs of the Mullen family, few of whom he ever saw at Sunday Mass, and decided to call in just to chivvy them along.

'Come in, Father,' said Katy Mullen. 'It's a pleasure to have you call. Have a cup of tea and a bun.'

Duly fed and watered, Father Murphy began the inquisition.

'I hope you're all still going to Sunday mass,' he said.

'Indeed we are,' replied Katy. 'Every Sunday regular – sometimes in the week as well.'

'And I hope you're all still saying the rosary together,' he furthered.

'Oh yes, Father,' said Mrs Mullen. 'Every evening without fail, twice at weekends.'

'And I trust you're still reading the Bible to these children?' said the priest.

'Oh yes, Father, every morning and every evening,' said Katy. 'Josephine, go and get that big book I'm always reading.'

Josephine returned with a Grattans Catalogue! (Oh well, some you win …)

If there was one problem in the parish it involved the constant rows between Sean and Bridie Flynn. Fearsome were their tempers and long were their memories.

So Friday evening saw them rowing over some small happening from months before. Bridie struck Sean with the phone – Sean countered with the back of his hand. Bridie came back with a broom handle across his shoulders. Sean grabbed the implement and pulled Bridie down the stairs. With the impetus of her fall, Sean spun her out of the open front door and into the street. He threw himself astride her winded frame and began slapping her across the face, just as Father Murphy came round the corner on his Friday visits.

Looking up and seeing the priest, Sean thought quickly and glowering at his prostrate spouse he roared: 'Now will you go to Mass?'

'Tis often so that the ways of the mere human are so vague that even men of the cloth find them hard to decipher.

Take the Jesuit preacher who decided to visit a small island off the coast of Connemara. The inhabitants numbered no more than a couple of dozen, but the Jesuit threw himself into the Lord's work with a vengeance. Having taken over the bar of the pub for Mass, and having delivered a fire and brimstone sermon, he questioned the congregation.

'How long is it since any of you had your

confessions heard?' he asked.

'Well, Father,' answered Brendan, the oldest inhabitant. 'It must be three years since the last priest was here.'

'Why didn't you make a trip to the mainland?' asked the priest.

'Well, Father,' said Brendan, 'the water between us and the mainland is very rough, and our boat is old and leaky. So you see if we've only venial sins to confess it's not worth the bother, and if we've mortal sins it's not worth the risk!'

A party of English tourists were taking in the sights of the west coast of Ireland (and surely when the sun is shining you wouldn't want to be anywhere else in the world). Having driven for a couple of hours the coach pulled up at a monastery where the holy men had prepared tea and cakes. After the snack the tourists were being shown around the historic building. Entering the kitchen they found a cleric slicing potatoes and dropping them into a pan of boiling fat.

'Oh I see,' said a smart-alec Englishman, 'you're obviously a chipmunk?'

'No,' was the reply, 'I'm the friar.'

So there stood the visiting missionary Father O'Sullivan, six feet tall, so red in the face he was nearly purple. As he stared from the pulpit he scanned the crowded church and, without warning, launched into an almighty tirade.

'Let me tell yez all this. Then I'll tell you no more,' he bellowed. 'The whole parish is going to hell. Everyone in this parish is going to hell!'

Stunned silence – open mouths – fear filled eyes – laughter. Laughter? Laughter? – from whom? Laughter from a little old man in the front row.

'The whole parish is going to hell. Every man, woman and child is going to hell. No escape, yez are all doomed.'

Silence – well, almost. All were transfixed except our little friend at the front. He was almost in hysterics.

'Didn't you hear me?' said Father O'Sullivan. 'I said the whole parish is going to hell.'

'I know,' said the old man, 'but I'm from the next parish, Father.'

So little Eamonn had returned from Sunday School and his mother asked what he'd learned that day.

'Well,' he said, 'Father O'Malley told us how Moses led the Israelites out of Egypt and into the Promised Land.'

'Indeed,' said Mother. 'And what exactly happened?'

'Well,' went on the little fellow. 'Moses got all the people together and loaded them into buses, lorries and cars. They drove off into the desert at night time and it wasn't till the morning that the Pharaoh found out they'd gone. When he realized what happened he was angry and he gathered all his army together, tanks, half tracks, jeeps and everything. They chased after the Israelites and they caught them at the Red Sea. Moses had built a pontoon bridge and he'd thrown it across the water and his people were just starting to cross when the Egyptians came up firing their rockets and anti-tank missiles and completely destroyed the Pharaoh's army. Then the people crossed the bridge into the Promised Land.'

'Wow, what a story,' said the mother. 'Is that what Father O'Malley told you?'

'Well, no,' replied Eamon. 'Not quite. But the way Father O'Malley told the tale you'd never believe it!'

Father O'Flynn was visiting his flock trying to raise money for new bells at St Margaret's Church. Much as the parishioners tried to dodge him, he knew where all their hiding places were. Even the back room of Dooley's bar where he managed to pounce on Flanagan, Nolan and Dolan who were playing cards and putting the world to rights.

'Come on, boys, just a few quid all round would play for the bells. Sure you hardly notice it out of your gambling money.'

'Fair dos,' they thought, and up they tipped with the money.

Nolan gave £10.

Dolan gave £10.

But, because Mick Flanagan was well ahead, he gave £50.

'Thanks, lads. God bless you. See you at church on Sunday,' said the reverend father.

Sunday came, the bells rang out from 6 a.m. till the Angelus at noon. All the parish turned out to rejoice at the sound. All, that is, except Flanagan. Where could he be? Not ill, surely?

Father O'Flynn went to his house after lunch and found the man slumped in front of the TV.

'Why weren't you there to celebrate the bells?' asked the priest.

'Celebrate,' said Mick. 'Celebrate! After all the money I paid. What do I hear? From 6 a.m. the bells have never changed. Nolan, Dolan, not a word about Flanagan!'

I suppose if there's going to be a disaster then it's the ideal place to find a holy man – even better if you can find an archbishop. I hold no belief in this tale – but I do wish it *had* been true!

The plane had developed engine trouble and the pilot had collapsed while trying to control the steep dive. The passengers scrambled for safety, but they could only find three parachutes and there were four of them. What to do? It was hard to think for the noise of the big Texan yapping off about what he'd done in the war and how he'd succeeded in life and how he should be saved above all the others.

'Indeed that's true,' said the archbishop, 'you

should take one parachute.' Without further argument the American grabbed the chute and leaped out.

'And you, my dear,' said the holy man to the young nurse. 'You must be saved. Because you have so much to offer and so much to live for.' Out leapt the nurse with the second chute.

'And now,' said the archbishop. 'Now …'

'Wait a moment,' said the boy scout. 'There's only one chute left your eminence, and you must take it.'

'Indeed, my son, we will both be saved. There are two parachutes left,' said his grace.

'Two?' stuttered the boy scout. 'How so?'

'Simple,' said the archbishop. 'I gave the big-mouthed Yank your haversack!'

(Wouldn't you just *love* that to be true?)

Father O'Sullivan did like his golf. 'Twas the only earthly passion that he had and he unashamedly indulged in it whenever possible. Regrettably he had one minor defect in his personality that ill-equipped him for the game and that was his quick-fire temper. So rather than calm and tranquillize the holy man, the golf served to incense him to the nth degree.

One Tuesday morning in particular, while playing in the Curates Cup event he really went overboard, slinging clubs and constantly shouting 'Missed you, you swine!'

'Calm down,' said Reverend McGee. 'Sure the Almighty will lose his rag with you if he hears what you're shouting.'

This did nothing to stop O'Sullivan's rampant behaviour. He swung, he failed to connect:

'Missed you, you swine!' he screamed.

He readdressed the ball, swung, failed to connect, 'Missed you, you swine!' he bellowed.

'Think what you're saying,' said Reverend McGee, to no avail.

Again the club was swung, again a fresh air shot. 'Missed you – you swine!' roared O'Sullivan.

Just then the clouds parted, deep thunder was heard and a bolt of lightning struck Father McGee. And a voice from heaven called out:

'Missed you, you swine!'

I hope you've enjoyed this wee look at life through Irish eyes. It's wonderful to see how simple they make all things look and how pleasant a place the world is when they are part of it. Even goodbyes are a joy to hear when they are said with the lilting voice that only the true Gaels possess:

'May the moon that shines over Mayo, shine on ye and all about ye till I see you again.'

'May Saint Patrick keep watch on you day and night, and should he close his eyes may he keep half a one open just for you!' (I never *did* work that one out!!)

But, dear reader, let me leave you with my own farewell, learned at the knee of the most Irish of grandmothers – Biddie McGrath.

'May you be in heaven half an hour before the devil knows you're dead!'